Katherine Paterson

Twayne's United States Authors Series
Children's Literature

Ruth K. MacDonald, Editor

TUSAS 642

KATHERINE PATERSON.
Photograph by Jill Paton Walsh. Used by permission.

Katherine Paterson

Gary D. Schmidt
Calvin College

Twayne Publishers • New York
Maxwell Macmillan Canada • Toronto
Maxwell Macmillan International • New York Oxford Singapore Sydney

Twayne Publishers
Macmillan Publishing Company
866 Third Avenue
New York, New York 10022

Maxwell Macmillan Canada, Inc.
1200 Eglinton Avenue East
Suite 200
Don Mills, Ontario M3C 3N1

Library of Congress Cataloging-in-Publication Data

Schmidt, Gary D.
Katherine Paterson/by Gary D. Schmidt.
p. cm. — (Twayne's United States authors series. Children's literature)
Includes bibliographical references and index.
ISBN 0-8057-3951-3 (alk. paper)
1. Paterson, Katherine—Criticism and interpretation. 2. Children's stories, American—History and criticism. I. Title. II. Series.
PS3566.A779Z83 1994
813'.54—dc20 93-30343
CIP

The paper used in this publication meets the minimum requirements of American National Standard for Information Sciences—Permanence of Paper for Printed Library Materials. ANSI Z39.48-1984.

10 9 8 7 6 5 4 3 2 1

Printed in the United States of America.

For Robert H. Schmidt and Jeanne A. Schmidt

Do you remember the day we came back from climbing the dunes of Fire Island and stopped at a little bookstore? And do you remember that I found a copy of Howard Pyle's *The Merry Adventures of Robin Hood* and desired it with all the fierce desire that a six-year-old boy can have? "It's too old for you," you said. And when I insisted that it wasn't, you brought in the owner of the store as an ally. "It's too old for you," he said. But still I insisted that it wasn't. You looked at each other, then you looked at the book, then you looked at me. And you bought it. The owner of the bookstore shrugged his shoulders.

Well, it was too old for me. But I read it anyway, to prove it wasn't. And I have been reading it ever since, nigh unto three decades. It sits next to me now as I write this—the same copy that my parents bought for me from a little bookstore by Fire Island because they love me.

And now I have a chance to give a book to you, which I do, because I love you.

Contents

Preface

In her essay "Where Is Terabithia?" Katherine Paterson tells of a time when her husband, John, was working in a craft shop near Silver Bay, New York:

> At the same table where he was working on stained glass were an elderly woman friend of his and a girl of twelve or so whom he did not know, and who seemed totally absorbed in her work. John and Elsie were chatting as they worked, catching up on each other's activities over the winter, when Elsie mentioned that she had read *Jacob Have I Loved.* Never shy, John asked her how she had liked it. "Oh," she said, "I loved it, because I know the place." "I loved it," said the girl, "because I know the feeling."[1]

Between the two of them, Elsie and the young girl, they have pretty much described this study. On the one hand, Katherine Paterson is the consummate storyteller who crafts tales in which characters must deal with the most elemental of fears and hopes, in settings alternately blissful and beatific, terrifying and desperate. She wants her readers to know the place, to know where and how and why a story takes place, and how characters set in that place react out of their contexts. Whether the place is the island of Rass in the Chesapeake Bay, or Strathaven in southwestern Virginia, or the mills of Lowell, Massachusetts, or the mountains of China, or the islands of Japan, Paterson establishes a place within which a story may play out.

But Paterson is also anxious for her readers to "know the feeling." It would not be an easy matter to find a contemporary writer for children who is so explicit about her concern for the effects of her books on child and young adult readers. Few would affirm Sir Philip Sidney's dictum that literature is meant to delight and—here is the sticking point—teach. For Paterson this is an appropriate description. She wants her novels to bring good news to the downtrodden, to proclaim the possibility of hope. In the words of her National Book Award acceptance speech, she wants to be "a spy for hope."[2]

Paterson's novels typically bring characters along the road that Christian trod. They move through various distressing valleys, both of humiliation and of the shadow of death. They search for fathers, for families, for love and acceptance, for themselves. They recall the characters of Flannery O'Connor, who also find themselves caught in moments of distress and then find, like Paterson's characters, moments of grace. That moment may come in the building of a bridge, or in beginning to understand the implications of a carol or poem, or in resolving to live a life of burdens shared. For a Paterson book to work—for it to be effective for a child reader, or any reader—the reader must come to know the feeling.

In Paterson's novel *Of Nightingales That Weep* Takiko and Goro go through horrendous episodes, where one is almost raped and killed, while the other wishes that he could die. In the end they find each other and come by grace into love. The novel concludes with the birth of their first child, a girl they will love and worship. Perhaps it is ironic that this is an ending that Paterson had to fight for; her editor balked at the notion of a young woman marrying her stepfather.[3] But it is precisely the right ending: none of the pain of their earlier lives is washed away but is overshadowed by joy. This is an element of the hope that Paterson continually holds out to her readers. Pain will be overshadowed by joy.

This study begins with a biographical essay about Paterson's life, drawn from her essays as well as from an interview conducted in Barre, Vermont. The focus here is on her life as a storyteller; in her 1985 Zena Sutherland lecture she quipped that her speech should carry the title of the old hymn, "I Love to Tell the Story."[4] Those familiar with the hymn will see the appropriateness of the title. The balance of the book focuses on Paterson's works, which I have grouped somewhat chronologically but, more accurately, according to subject. Thus readers will find *Rebels of the Heavenly Kingdom* taking precedence over earlier works, since that novel is of such a piece with Paterson's early historical fiction.

In each critical discussion I focus on the elements of hope, for this theme is consistent; played out among various other melodies, it nevertheless marks each of her novels. If the critical technique verges closer to that of Matthew Arnold than that of recent critical schools, the tendency comes from my own wariness of the merely new. (Those willing to dismiss such an approach as something primeval might recall, in thinking of recent critical schools, the final lines of Shelley's "Ozymandias.") My interest is in how Paterson does what she does: tell stories. To talk about how they mean is to talk about how they are told. And this, I hope, is what this study will do.

Acknowledgments

The acknowledgments to a book three years in the making will inevitably be flawed because they can never truly chronicle the debts that the writer has incurred. But certainly I can begin with the greatest debt, and that is to Anne Stickney Schmidt, my wife. Yet again she has put up with all the vagaries of a writing project, listening, encouraging, suggesting, pointing to gaps, and in general being the fine reader that she is. I thank her for all the many gifts she has given to this work.

My thanks also to Katherine Paterson, who took the awful news that someone was going to be writing a book about her with grace and aplomb, and who was willing to have me, Anne, and our four children descend on her between the wedding of one of her children and the packing off of another to school halfway across the country. My blessed.

As always, my debt to Conrad Bult, reference librarian of Calvin College Library, is enormous. His willingess to produce survey maps of Virginia, to point the way to books about Chinese and Japanese history, to find sources for the most obscure topics is evidence of his enormous graciousness. My thanks as well to Kathy Struck, also of Calvin College Library, for filling all the many interlibrarian loan requests, finding texts that probably no one else could ever have found.

That the book was ever converted from penciled legal pads and the worn type of my 1953 Royal to the clean look of a computer screen is due to the secretary of Calvin College's English Department, Sherry Smith, as well as her assistants, Lisa Spoelhof and Christine Weeber. My thanks to them for putting up with all of my unreasonable and exacting requests with such perfect serenity.

This study was funded in part by a sabbatical from Calvin College, and my acknowledgment of that carries with it my thanks to my college and my department for their continuing support.

Chronology

1932	Katherine Clements Womeldorf born in Tsing-Tsiang Pu, China, on 31 October to George Raymond Womeldorf and Mary (Goetchius) Womeldorf.
1937	The Womeldorfs are refugeed from China; move to Virginia for one year.
1938	The Womeldorfs return to China to resume missionary duties.
1940	The Womeldorfs return to the United States, refugeed once again.
1954	Katherine graduates from King College, Bristol, Tennessee.
1954–1955	Teaches public school in Lovettsville, Virginia.
1957	Graduates with an M.A. from the Presbyterian School of Christian Education.
1957–1959	Attends Naganuma School of the Japanese Language, Kobe, Japan.
1957–1962	Is missionary in Japan under the Presbyterian Church, U.S.A., the Board of World Missions, Nashville, Tennessee.
1962	Marries John Barstow Paterson. Graduates with M.R.E. from the Union Theological Seminary.
1963–1965	Teaches sacred studies and English at Pennington School for Boys, Pennington, New Jersey.

1965 The Paterson family moves to Tacoma Park, Virginia.

1966 *Who Am I?*

1973 *Justice for All People. To Make Men Free. The Sign of the Chrysanthemum.*

1974 *Of Nightingales That Weep.*

1976 *The Master Puppeteer.*

1977 The Paterson family moves to Norfolk, Virginia. *Bridge to Terabithia.* Paterson wins National Book Award and Newbery Honor for *The Master Puppeteer.*

1978 *The Great Gilly Hopkins.* Wins first Newbery Award for *Bridge to Terabithia.*

1979 *Angels and Other Strangers.* Wins National Book Award and Newbery Honor for *The Great Gilly Hopkins.*

1980 *Jacob Have I Loved.*

1981 Translator, *The Crane Wife.* Wins second Newbery Award for *Jacob Have I Loved. Gates of Excellence: On Reading and Writing Books for Children.*

1983 *Rebels of the Heavenly Kingdom.* Wins Silver Medallion from the University of Southern Mississippi.

1985 *Come Sing, Jimmy Jo.*

1986 The Paterson family moves to Barre, Vermont. *Consider the Lilies: Plants of the Bible.* With John Paterson.

1987 Translator, *The Tongue-cut Sparrow.*

1988 *Park's Quest.*

1989 *The Spying Heart: More Thoughts on Reading and Writing Books for Children.*

1990 *The Tale of the Mandarin Ducks.*

1991 *Lyddie. The Smallest Cow in the World.*

1992 *The King's Equal.* "Asia in 1492," in *The World in 1492.*

1994 *Flip-Flop Girl.*

1.

Gathering Stories Along the Way

On a warm, August day last summer, my wife, Anne, and I crossed the mountains of Vermont to Barre, a small town with a gazeboed square filled, that night, with the sounds of a Scottish Festival. In the evening we climbed a small but steep hill to a house whose wide boards and square, no-nonsense construction suggested its age and New England heritage. There we met Katherine Paterson, who invited us for a cup of tea, who endured all the questions that pried into her writings, and who laughed and told stories. The more I remember that evening, the more I remember listening mostly to the stories, a cup of tea in hand, cozy in the couch, my pencil and pad forgotten in the stories.

When one comes to consider the work of Katherine Paterson, one comes first of all to consider story. In accepting the National Book Award in 1977, Paterson made her principal point by reference to story:

> I do write for children. For my own four children and for others who are faced with the question of whether they dare to become adult, responsible for their own lives and the lives of others. . . . I want to become a spy like Joshua and Caleb. I have crossed the river and tangled with a few giants, but I want to go back and say to those who are hesitating, "Don't be afraid to cross

> over. The promised land is worth possessing and we are not alone." I want to be a spy for hope.[1]

Leaving aside here for the moment the theme of hope—a theme that dominates Paterson's work—what is significant in this approach is the use of the story of the first tentative and nervous penetration into the Promised Land. To be a spy, to encourage hope for a young reader, Paterson tells stories. Stories of lost souls and found souls, stories of lonely souls and comforting souls, souls of those who have given themselves away and souls who have been given the gift of themselves.

Paterson's stories come out of her experience and her immediate concerns. Perhaps they do not so much tell her life—and the life of her family—as reflect it in what must be on some level a darkened mirror to her readers. When one reads *Bridge to Terabitha* one comes willy-nilly to the story of Lisa Hill, the close friend of Paterson's son David; Lisa was killed by a lightning bolt and an apparently capricious God who seemed somehow and for some reason to be punishing David. *The Sign of the Chrysanthemum,* about a young boy searching desperately—and unsuccessfully—for his father, was written during a time when Paterson's elder daughter, Lin, who is adopted, was searching for her biological parents. *The Great Gilly Hopkins,* about a foster child, is dedicated to Mary, whom the Patersons had adopted. The novel came about after an emergency call asking the Patersons to serve as foster parents. *The Master Puppeteer* focuses on the relationship between two young boys, Jiro and Kinshi, who, Paterson acknowledges, resemble her elder son, John.

None of this is important to the child reader coming to these stories; he or she will not know about Lisa Hill, or perhaps even guess at the meaning of that book's dedications. But the connections to Paterson's experience suggest something about how she approaches story. She has divided her influences into a trinity that matches much of her biography: her childhood in China, her years living in the South, and her Presbyterian background.[2] It is telling that the influences she describes are so entirely biographical, rather than, say, literary. In fact, the authors she remembers reading as a child—A. A. Milne, Kenneth Graham, J. R. R. Tolkien, Martha Farquharson (the author of the Elsie Dinsmore novels), Kate Seredy, Robert Lawson, and Rachel Fields[3]—are about as far afield from the work of Katherine Paterson as one might imagine. "I write novels that have the whole scope of human life," she asserts, and so writers like Charles Dickens and Flannery O'Connor are truer models. If one would search for works among children's books, Paterson herself sees works like Francis Burnett's *The Secret Garden* and Marjorie Rawlings's *The Yearling* as "closer to what I try to do. Of course I am influenced by what I read and see. It is all a part of who I am, and as a writer I am sifting it" (Interview).

It is to Paterson's life that one must first turn to understand her work. Many of her childhood and formative years were spent in the South, which, she suggests, has a tradition of fine storytelling. And reading the Bible through all these years also contributed to her storytelling: "Eudora Welty once said that 'Southerners do have, they've inherited, a narrative sense of human destiny.'. . . [O]f course that's why the South is known as the Bible Belt. We in the South were raised on this book that has a beginning, a middle and an end—a coherent plot, with wonderful, richly human characters, a vivid setting, and a powerful theme."[4] Paterson's is a life filled with the gathering of story, as though, like Louise, God in heaven had been preparing her to be a storyteller all along.

Paterson was born of an All Hallows' Eve in 1932, in Tsing-Tsiang Pu, in Jiangsu Province, on China's eastern coast, fronting the Yellow Sea. Today it is a province known for the cities of Nanking and Shanghai, as well as the Yangtze River that winds through it. During the first decade of Paterson's life, however, that province would be known instead for the continual fighting between the Communist and Kuomintang forces that went on there. In fact, Paterson could hardly have been born into a more tumultuous decade.

Nanking was the seat of Kuomintang government, and at Paterson's birth that government was halfway through its tenuous hold in that city. It was established in 1927 following a purge of Chinese Communists, but later that year Mao Tse-tung began his guerrilla warfare techniques in Kiangsi province, not far to the west. In the years just before Paterson's birth that group grew quickly, both in number and in the land it controlled. It would not be long until the beginning of the Long March, which began when Paterson was just turning two; it concluded when she was turning three and Mao Tse-tung was emerging as the dominant Communist leader.

Just seven months before Paterson's birth, Japan had annexed Manchuria and founded a state they called Manchukuo. Five years of fighting between the Communist and Kuomintang forces were to pass before an uneasy truce was called to fight the Anti-Japanese War, which would last until the end of World War II. Jiangsu Province would see much of the fighting in this war. Though the fighting began near Beijing, the Japanese opened a second front near Shanghai just a month before Paterson's fifth birthday, and three months later, in December of 1937, they had stormed through the province and taken Nanking.

It was into this troubled world that Paterson's parents, George Raymond and Mary (Goetchius) Womeldorf traveled as missionaries for the Southern Presbyterian Church. Her father, raised among the independent and hard-working farmers of Virginia's Shenandoah Valley, had fought with the French in World War I, receiving for this work a dosage of gas and the loss of his right leg. When he turned to travel to China, now as a missionary rather than a soldier, he brought with him some of the qualities that enabled him to survive the warfare that killed so many millions. Years later Paterson wrote that "he was, I believe, as ideally suited as any Westerner to go to China. He was intelligent, hard-working, almost fearless, absolutely stoical, and amazingly humble, with the same wonderful sense of humor found in many Chinese. Not only was he capable of learning the language and enduring the hardships of his chosen life, but he was also incapable of seeing himself in the title role of Great White Deliverer" ("Sounds," 700). It is tempting to look for characters like this in Paterson's novels; Fukuji of *The Sign of the Chrysanthemum* comes to mind, as does Goro the artisan of *Of Nightingales That Weep*.

To read of Paterson's life during these years is almost inevitably to make comparisons to the childhood of Jean Fritz, whose *Homesick: My Own Story* tells of her life in China up until 1927, when she was 12 and her family was forced to flee.[5] Perhaps the most glaring distinction between Paterson's and Fritz's childhoods is that while Fritz lived in a British quarter, Paterson lived in a school complex where most of her neighbors were Chinese. Her father, she writes, rode with a close Chinese companion, another Christian minister, "from village to village, sleeping on the straw in flea-ridden pigsties because they were the best accommodation some friendly farmer could offer. Where there was famine—as there too often was—they went with food, and where there was plague or disease, they went with medicine" ("Sounds," 700). The result was a childhood lived in very close proximity to the Chinese culture. This was to influence all of Paterson's writing, from the earliest historical fiction to the later retelling of folktales. But it was also to influence the course of much of her later life:

> What this meant for me was that when I went to Japan many years later, I had, through no virtue of my own, an attitude towards the Orient that most Westerners, especially the Americans I met there, seemed to lack. I knew that I had come to a civilization far older than my own, to a language that after a lifetime of study I would still be just beginning to grasp, to a people whose sense of beauty I could only hope to appreciate but never to duplicate. ("Sounds," 700–701)

With the onset of World War II and the Japanese invasion, the Womeldorf family was refugeed twice back to the United States. The family's flights from China were to mark the beginning of many moves. In 1937 they returned to the United States for the first time, moving to Lynchburg, Virginia, and then to Richmond. "I hated America," wrote Paterson in 1978. "When I was in the first grade I didn't get any valentines. I don't think I was disliked. I was totally overlooked."[6] This incident, too, was to become part of the gathering of stories: "My mother grieved over this event until her death, asking me once why I didn't write a story about the time I didn't get any valentines. 'But mother,' I said, 'all my stories are about the time I didn't get any valentines.'"[7]

The Womeldorfs ventured back to China in 1938, but it was too dangerous to return to their original home, and only her father was able to go back to the city. Paterson witnessed Japanese soldiers practicing a mock invasion: "I was out playing and heard this blood-chilling sound. Soldiers wearing only a loincloth and carrying guns with bayonets were coming up our yard. I grabbed my little sister's hand and ran for all I was worth" (cited in Buckly, 370). The family stayed in Shanghai, living mostly in the British section. For the first time in Paterson's life in China she was separated from the culture. Once again she saw herself as apart from a culture; perhaps her loss of her language skills accentuated this feeling. It is perhaps not too large a leap of the imagination to see in Paterson's early sense of separateness many of the dilemmas of her characters, who also see themselves as separate.

The second flight from China represented a permanent move away for the Womeldorfs. It would be years before Paterson had the opportunity to return to China and Japan. When she returned to Japan as a missionary, she had to overcome her childhood fear of and anger at the Japanese, as well as her resentment over being teased by American children and called a "Jap" since she had been born somewhere in the east. But when she returned again in 1973 to do research in the Japanese puppet theater, she was coming back to a people and land that she loved. Her return to China waited until 1981, when she went back to do the research for *Rebels of the Heavenly Kingdom,* her only novel set in the land of her birth.

Like Jean Fritz, Paterson found her childhood marked by a sense that she was somehow different from those around her. This was not alleviated by 15 moves between 1937 and 1950, taking the family from China to Virginia to North Carolina to West Virginia and Tennessee. The Womeldorf family returned for the second time from China in 1940 when Paterson was eight, and her reception at the Calvin H. Wiley School in Winston-Salem North Carolina was not atypical of her school experiences:

> I had only recently gotten off a boat that had brought us refugeeing from China. I spoke English with a British accent and wore clothes out of a missionary barrel. Because children are somewhat vague about geography, my classmates knew only that I had come from somewhere over there and decided I was, if not a Japanese spy, certainly suspect, so they called me, in the friendly way that children have, "Jap." The only thing I could do anything about was the accent. Although I have since that time lived in five states and one foreign country, I still speak like a North Carolinian. ("Dinsmore," 101)

The humor—"in the friendly way that children have"—suggests a pain that has not entirely vanished. "As a child, I was so much an outsider," she recalls (Interview). It is not hard to imagine Gilly Hopkins as an adult speaking this way about her past. It may explain why so few of Paterson's characters have strong friends, what Anne of Green Gables would call "bosom" friends. It may also explain why so many adults figure hugely in her novels, in a field where adult characters are often subordinated.

One result of that sense of separateness was a love of reading, though certainly in one to the story born this love would have developed willy-nilly. She had only a few books when she was quite young and remembers particularly the poems of A. A. Milne and the gentle fantasy of *The Wind in the Willows*. She began to write, publishing her first poem in the *Shanghai American,* the school newspaper, when she was only seven. By the next year she was trying her hand at Elsie Dinsmore imitations. When she was nine and living in North Carolina she discovered the library, perhaps first as a refuge from the ministrations of the playground bullies. There she found Robert Lawson, Rachel Fields, and Kate Seredy, as well as a stern but understanding librarian who nourished her reading as well as her respect for and love of books in general—not only the text, but the physical book itself ("Dinsmore," 102–3). By the fifth grade she had begun to sense her calling: "I was very verbal and started writing plays. The kids respected this. I loved acting and was the evil fairy in *The Sleeping Beauty*" (cited in Buckley, 370).

Never since her earliest days had Paterson lived in one place for as long as she would stay in Bristol, Tennessee, where she was to attend King College from 1950 to 1954 by the foothills of the Great Smoky Mountains. She was to graduate summa cum laude from that school, after being immersed in the work of John Donne, Shakespeare, Sophocles, and Gerard Manley Hopkins, whose name Paterson would borrow for one of her own characters. She also read the *Narnia Chronicles,* which were being published during those years. When one thinks of the complex diction and the entangled style of Donne and Hopkins, or the strong, dominant narrative voice of C. S. Lewis's *Narnia Chronicles,* it seems difficult to find in this reading any formative tendencies. But Paterson found it useful to examine and even imitate the voices of these writers, concluding that "an apprenticeship imitating the masters of the English language was bound to have a beneficial effect."[8]

Paterson was still 12 years away from her first book and almost 20 years away from her first novel, but already she saw in her writing an apprenticeship. It was, however, an unconscious apprenticeship, if those two words are not self-contradictory. Two years after graduation she was asked by a professor if she had ever considered being a writer. "'No,' I replied, swelling with twenty-four-year-old pomposity. 'I wouldn't want to add another mediocre writer to the world.' 'But maybe that's what God is calling you to be,'" replied the professor. One hears here the voice of Joseph Wojtkiewicz, calling the reluctant Louise to recognize the hand of God in heaven, who had been raising her for the valley all of her life. Paterson was as reluctant to accept this vocation, it seems, as Louise. But Paterson recognized one other thing from that important conversation: "If I wasn't willing to risk mediocrity, I'd never accomplish anything" ("Excellence," 2).

Paterson did return to school, but not for her writing; she instead became interested in education. After graduation from King College she traveled to Lovettsville, situated on the banks of the Cneactin Creek in northern Virginia and surrounded by towns with evocative names like Round Hill, Lucketts, Clarkes Gap, and, only 30 miles away as the crow flies, Shanghai. There she taught for a year in a small elementary school but left in the fall of 1956 to attend the Presbyterian School of Christian Education, not far away from Lovettsville in Richmond. After a year she received a master's degree in English Bible and then decided to do something that would have seemed impossible to her in her childhood: she would go to Japan. She recalls,

> What made it possible for me to go to Japan at all was a close friend I had in graduate school, a Japanese woman pastor who persuaded me that despite the war, I would find a home in Japan, if I would give the Japanese people a chance. And she was right. In the course of four years I was set fully free from my deep childish hatred. I truly loved Japan, and one of the most heart-warming compliments I ever received came from a Japanese man I worked with who said to me one day that someone had told him that I had been born in China. Was that true? I assured him it was. "I knew it," he said "I've always known there was something Oriental about you." ("Sounds," 701)

Perhaps the fellow was right; certainly in the four years she lived there she came to see Japan in a very different way; she would set three of her early novels there, all marked especially by a love of Japan's history and land.

In the fall of 1957 Paterson enrolled at the Naganuma School of Japanese Language in Kobe, just across the Inland Sea from Shikoku Island, where she lived. (If she had traveled west across the Inland Sea instead of north to Kobe, she would have arrived at Hiroshima, a vivid reminder of the war.) Shikoku Island, the smallest of Japan's major islands, is dominated by large rural areas. Paterson served as a Christian education assistant for 11 pastors in these rural areas, again becoming part of an Asian culture. In fact, after four years she found once again that when she returned to America she returned as an alien. Back home in Virginia—if "home" is the right word—she found that her family did not seem to understand who she was: "The reason I thought my family didn't know me was that they didn't know me in Japanese."[9] Yet again Paterson seemed to be set apart, this time from her own family—an experience that Jess would understand in *Bridge to Terabithia* and James in *Come Sing, Jimmy Jo.* She explains, "You see, in those four years I had become a different person. I had not only learned new ways to express myself, I had new thoughts to express. I had come by painful experience to a conclusion that linguists now advance: language is not simply the instrument by which we communicate thought. The language we speak will shape the thought and feelings themselves" ("Words," 8). Jess's attempts to communicate through his art, James's attempts to communicate through his music, and the failure of both to reach their families recalls what must have been a painful time in Paterson's life.

Paterson soon left Virginia and traveled to New York City, which probably seemed as strange and exotic a cultural change as moving from Lovettsville to Shikoku Island. There she accepted a fellowship at Union Theological Seminary where she took her second master's degree, this time in religious education, completing it in 1962. It was a degree that would prepare her for her first professional writing assignment.

1962 would also see a significant change in Paterson's life, as she met and married John Barstow Paterson, a Presbyterian minister. It was not long before she had four children—two natural sons, John and David, and two adopted daughters, Elizabeth Polin, who is Chinese, and Mary Katherine Nah-he-sah-pe-che-a, who is Apache Kiowa. A busy, young household is not an easy situation in which to craft a style, especially one so different from any of her favorite authors. Her novels, she writes, "might have happened sooner had I had a room of my own and fewer children, but somehow I doubt it. For as I look back on what I have written, I can see that the very persons who have taken away my time and space are those who have given me something to say" ("Excellence," 3).

In 1964 she could not have had that perspective, however, and it was in that year that she began work on her first book, *Who Am I?,* written as part of a church school curriculum and published by John Knox Press in 1966. Twenty-five years later she would credit that book with beginning her life as a writer. She was able to write while staying at home, so the profession seemed practical.

And this particular book had the added attraction of combining her expertise in Christian education with her love of story.

Over the next seven years Paterson continued to write. The family moved to Tacoma Park, Maryland, where John was the minister of Tacoma Park Presbyterian Church and where Paterson wrote *Justice for All People* and *To Make Men Free,* both published in 1973, the first by Friendship Press and the second by John Knox Press. If Jess Aarons were to try to find these today, he would shake his head and mutter, "Lord." Both of these slim and difficult to come by volumes are interesting today not only for the material they present but especially for the way in which they present it. In *Justice for All People,* for example, Paterson focuses on the Middle East to examine the Christian conception of justice:

> People have always searched for justice, but usually they have been most concerned with justice when feeling that they have been wronged. Rarely does one look for justice when he or she is the wrongdoer. Our Christian faith involves us in the search for justice for our neighbors as well as for ourselves, for our enemies as well as for our friends. It also demands that we submit our own actions to the perfect judgment of God, so that when we have commtted injustice against others we will recognize this fact and with God's help seek to remedy the situations that have been caused or aggravated by our wrong-doing. We must be just because God is just.[10]

To accomplish the goals of the study, Paterson suggests techniques that are typically hers: she tells stories and perhaps recalling her childhood interest in drama—she drafts plays. These are taken from the Bible, from Arab folklore, from contemporary experiences of children, and from contemporary history. In part this particular book is interesting as a foreshadowing of Paterson's work in *The World in 1492* (1992), but in its use of story and dramatic situation to explore complex human issues it points more closely to Paterson's novels.

While Paterson was writing for the Presbyterian Church, U.S.A., and the National Council of Churches, she was also working on fiction, though none of it was published. With the encouragement of her husband, she began to write stories that were read at Tacoma Park Presbyterian Church on successive Christmas Eves; perhaps when Paterson first began writing these she did not anticipate that they would one day be published, but in 1979 they were, as *Angels and Other Strangers,* a collection of nine short stories about Christmas.

But it was in 1973 that the important breakthrough came, a year in which Paterson had three books published, one of which, *The Sign of the Chrysanthemum,* was to point the way for her future work. It had been written at the pace of a chapter a week for an adult education class, then had endured two years of rejection until accepted from a pile of unsolicited manuscripts at Crowell Publishers. It received mixed, though mostly favorable reviews; in retrospect, it seems to have provided the moment for all the gathered stories, all the gathered impressions, all the strong feelings of her own childhood to coalesce around a tale. Two more novels set in Japan quickly followed: *Of Nightingales That Weep,* published the next year, and a mystery novel, *The Master Puppeteer,* published in 1976. Each focuses on a protagonist who at least begins as a child but who finds, in the swirl of political and cultural events, an opportunity for growth.

> After I had written *The Sign of the Chrysanthemum* . . . one of my good friends who is an ardent feminist asked me to make my next book about a girl, a strong person who overcomes many odds and would serve as a role model for my friend's daughter and maybe my own two daughters as well. It started out all right, but the more I listened to the story, the more I realized that my strong girl was also selfish and vain and would be brought low by her flaws as well as exalted by her strengths. She turned, you see, in the course of the story, into a human being, set in a specific time in history and in actual geographical location, both of which conspired against her budding feminism.[11]

The result is a novel about a real character, rather than about a cause. It is perhaps this quality more than any other that led to

Paterson's first major award in children's literature: the National Book Award for *The Master Puppeteer,* presented to her in 1977.

In 1977, after 13 years in Tacoma Park, the Patersons moved to Norfolk, Virginia, where John took up the pastorate of Lafayette Presbyterian Church, a post he held until August of 1986. Here Paterson began working on *Bridge to Terabithia,* perhaps the most moving and painful of her books. It began with the death of her son David's close friend, but was also written in the context of Paterson's brush with cancer and mortality:

> After a few false starts, thirty-two smudged pages emerged, which made me feel that perhaps there might be a book after all. In a flush of optimism I moved to the typewriter and pounded out a few dozen more, only to find myself growing colder and colder with each page until I was totally frozen. The time had come for my fictional child to die, and I could not let it happen.
>
> I caught up on my correspondence, I rearranged my bookshelves, I even cleaned the kitchen—anything to keep the inevitable from happening. And then one day a friend asked, as friends will, "How is the new book coming?" and I blurted out—"I'm writing a book in which a child dies, and I can't let her die. I guess," I said, "I can't face going through Lisa's death again."
>
> "Katherine," she said, looking me in the eye, for she is a true friend, "I don't think it's Lisa's death you can't face. I think it's yours."
>
> I went straight home to my study and closed the door. If it was my death I could not face, then by God, I would face it. I began in a kind of fever, and in a day I had written the chapter, and within a few weeks I had completed the draft, the cold sweat pouring down my arms.[12]

It is hard to read this account and not think of Gerard Manley Hopkins's poem "Margaret, Are You Grieving?," which concludes with Margaret's awareness of her mortality: "It is the blight man was born for, / It is Margaret you mourn for." But it is also evident from Paterson's own accounting of the genesis of *Bridge to Terabithia* how the gathering of stories is crucial to understanding her novels. *Bridge to Terabithia* is a merger of stories from her past, her son's experience, and her present, all subordinated to the larger story. (It is also to be noted that the account of the beginning of the novel is itself a dramatic story.)

Even Terabithia itself represents this merger, coming from the combination of the pine woods behind her North Carolina childhood home and woods the Paterson family discovered during a roadside stop while on vacation. The name Terabithia comes from C. S. Lewis's *The Voyage of the Dawn Treader,* or perhaps from the terebinth tree mentioned in the Old Testament.[13]

Bridge to Terabithia won the 1978 Newbery Award, and her next book, *The Great Gilly Hopkins,* earned a Newbery Honor and the one after that, *Jacob Have I Loved* (published only three years after *Bridge to Terabithia*), a second Newbery Award. In the middle of these books Paterson became the American nominee for the Hans Christian Andersen Award in 1980. The authorial winner that year was Bohumil Riha, from Czechoslovakia, but ironically it was Suekichi Akaba from Japan who won as an illustrator; he would later illustrate the retellings of two Japanese folktales that Paterson translated: *The Tongue-cut Sparrow* and *The Crane Wife.* In 1986 Paterson was nominated for the Laura Ingalls Wilder Award; it went that year to another refugee from China, Jean Fritz.

The 1980s were busy years for Paterson, as her books continued to garner impressive awards, from the Newbery Award to Kansas's William Allen White Award, and she continued to produce new novels, many dealing with similar themes, but each characterized by strong central characters and vivid settings. *The Great Gilly Hopkins* was published in 1978 and set in a town modeled on Tacoma Park. *Jacob Have I Loved* was published in 1980 and set on the islands of the Chesapeake Bay, not far from Norfolk, perhaps inspired in terms of its setting by William W. Warner's *Beautiful Swimmers: Watermen, Crabs and the Chesapeake Bay,* published only four years earlier.[14] *Rebels of the Heavenly Kingdom* followed in 1983, in which Paterson was able, for the first and only time, to set her work in China. *Come Sing, Jimmy Jo* came two years later, set in West Virginia, and then *Park's Quest,* set in Washington, D.C., and the fictional town of Strathaven, in the southwestern corner of Virginia.

In 1986 Katherine and John Paterson collaborated on their first book together: *Consider the Lilies.* Paterson would eventually contribute to several books, such as *Once upon a Time: Celebrating the Magic in Children's Books in Honor of the Twentieth Anniversary of Reading Is Fundamental* (1986)[15]; *Face to Face* (1990),[16] a collection of stories by American and Soviet writers, to which Paterson contributed a selection from *Park's Quest*; and *The World in 1492* (1992),[17] to which Paterson added a discussion of Asia in the late fifteenth century. *Consider the Lilies* is the only work she has co-authored, and it must be said that the book is as much the work of the illustrator, Anne Ophelia Dowden, as it is that of the Patersons.

The premise behind *Consider the Lilies* is that the biblical writers used the familiar to talk about the unfamiliar, the physical to talk about the spiritual. "People can best visualize unimaginable things by means of things they know," the Patersons write. "The writers of the Bible understood this. That is why in telling us stories about God's mysterious dealings with the world, they have used what we can see and touch and smell and hear and taste to point us to truths beyond our experience."[18]

The book is divided into sections entitled Revelation, Necessity, and Celebration, suggesting the differing roles that fauna might have played in illustrating God's workings among his people. Each section includes several plants and the scriptural passages in which they are mentioned. The book is bounded by references to the Tree of Life, both that in Eden and that in the New Jerusalem. But perhaps what binds the book even more solidly is a sense of story once again; the plants tell, in a very different way, the story of God and His chosen people.

The olive, for example, suggests Revelation, in that it points to something in the nature of God and how His plan of salvation is worked out. The date, fig, and pomegranate are included under Necessity, suggesting God's provision for His needy people. Myrrh and Frankincense and Rock Rose are included under Celebration, in that these expensive and fragrant resins were precious gifts. The book, then, is a mixture of genres. In one sense this is a retelling of biblical stories, sometimes through close adherence to a text, but sometimes through an interpretive retelling. In another sense it is an information book attempting to identify the plants mentioned in biblical passages. But in its strongest sense, *Consider the Lilies* is a devotional text, suggesting ways that God Himself tells his stories.

Around the time of *Consider the Lilies* the Patersons moved from Norfolk to Barre, Vermont, where John took up the pastorate of the First Presbyterian Church of Barre, a position he still holds. Paterson had by this time become a frequent contributor to journals like *Horn Book,* a book reviewer for *Washington Post Book World,* and a member of the editorial board of *Writer,* so her writing commitments had become quite heavy. The move to Barre was an extraordinary change; to move from the coast of Virginia to the Green Mountains of central Vermont is among the most dramatic changes one can make in the continental United States. And with this change came new directions in Paterson's work. *The Crane Wife* had been a project proposed by Morrow Publishers, but that same publisher had turned down the chance to have *The Tongue-cut Sparrow* translated, feeling that the illustrations would not appeal to an American audience. Paterson, however, liked the story very much, as well as the humor of the illustrations. While visiting Japan in 1985, she met the publisher of the Japanese edition, who sent her a copy of the book and asked her if she would be interested in translating it. Paterson did so and showed it to her editor, who accepted the book enthusiastically (Interview).

Paterson's translation of *The Tongue-cut Sparrow,* published in 1987, was followed by a retelling of another Japanese folktale, *The Tale of the Mandarin Ducks,* illustrated by Leo and Diane Dillon and published in 1990. Her history of Asia in the fifteenth century was published in 1992 in a volume that included an essay on Europe by Jean Fritz, whose early life seems to have paralleled Paterson's. In that same year Paterson wrote *The King's Equal,* an original fairy tale. Even her novel writing found a new setting, as she attended a Women's History Project for Vermont's bicentennial celebration and was deeply moved by the reading of letters from Vermont farm girls who had gone to Lowell, Massachusetts, to work in the textile mills. She then wrote what may be her darkest novel, *Lyddie,* setting it in Vermont and in Lowell during the 1840s.

Ray Bradbury has written about his own use of his past to write novels:

> When I began to write *Dandelion Wine,* first I rummaged through my mind for words that could describe my personal nightmares, fears of night, and time from my childhood. Then I took a long look at the green apple trees and the old house I was born in, and the house next door where my grandparents lived, and all the lawns of the summers I grew up in, and I began to try words for all that. I shaped stories from these.
>
> What you have in *Dandelion Wine* then is a gathering of dandelions from all those years, all the summers of my childhood in one book. The wine metaphor that appears again and again in these pages is wonderfully apt. I was gathering images all my life, storing them away, and forgetting them. Somehow I had to send myself back, with words as catalysts, to open the memories out and see what they had to offer.[19]

This is the process of Katherine Paterson, though perhaps it is not so self-conscious as that of Ray Bradbury. "There is as much loose talk these days," she writes, "about creativity as there is about self-expression. But those of us who are mortal do not create ex nihilo—out of nothing—any more than we simply express ourselves" ("Aim," 326). The novels of Katherine Paterson are gathered dandelions, shaped by the art of the novelist, chosen, turned, and examined until they fit, woven into bright dandelion tapestries to make an artistic whole.

Sitting with Katherine Paterson that August evening, perhaps the thing my wife and I saw as most evident about Paterson's relationship to her work was how passionately real it was to her. When I suggested to her that part of the pain of *Lyddie*'s ending was her isolation, how her courageous decision meant that she would not marry Luke Stevens, Paterson's denial was emphatic: "She'll come back to marry him. She goes to get her education, and then she'll come back and marry and have children. And maybe she'll do what many of these girls did: start a library." When I suggested that *Lyddie* was probably her most painful book, she thought for a moment and then shook her head and said, "No, Lyddie's tough. Even when Rachel leaves, you know she'll get through it because she's gotten through everything else. It's not her fault that her life was so hard. I think *Jacob Have I Loved* is my most painful novel. Louise's life was so hard because she made it hard" (Interview). The tone of her voice carries the pain that she feels for Louise.

There is a sense here that these characters are very real; this is certainly the case when Paterson is writing her books: "When I'm writing, I am not thinking about anything but the story. There is a totally different world that even I'm not in" (Interview). But clearly this reality continues. She did not say that it *may* be that Lyddie would come back: she *does* come back and she *does* marry and she *does* find a fulfillment that she had been so without. When she asked at the end of her Newbery Award acceptance speech, "Oh MayBelle, will you ever make a queen?" ("Newbury," 366), she was not merely reaching for a rhetorical effect but asking a question with integrity.

What Paterson does in her novels is to present the reader with a small slice of a character's life. Perhaps it is a slice that covers some years, as with, say, Wang Lee or Louise. But it may be a short period of time, as with Jess, or the many characters of *Angels and Other Strangers*. Often what has come before is indicated. And most often what is still ahead of these characters is suggested. But there is a real sense that we have only a small portion of the whole to look at, though Paterson indicates that somehow this small portion will be determinative in a very real way.

"Who you are and what you believe will come out willy-nilly in your writing" (Interview), suggests Paterson, and perhaps that is why Paterson's novels conclude with hope. They are not conventionally happy endings: Leslie does really die, Jimmy Jo's family is not yet healed, Park's father has lost the trust and perhaps the love of Park's mother; and Gilly's mother has not come with love and grace (though, Paterson insists, if you knew Courtney's story, you would love her and cry for her too) (Interview). But they are endings that point toward grace. You cannot read Katherine Paterson without feeling the weight of Flannery O'Connor's influence: characters experience moments of grace and revelation that will determine the rest of their lives. This is true of Paterson's characters, too, whether it be Gilly meeting Trotter, Jess meeting Leslie, Wang Lee meeting Mei Lin, or Muna meeting Fukuji. And these examples suggest that in Paterson's work grace comes mediated through persons, who knows how.

And, having gathered stories along the way, Paterson comes as yet another mediator, yet another spy for hope.

2.

The Search for Hope: The Early Historical Fiction

Paterson set her earliest novels in a part of the world she knew well: the Orient. Her first three novels were set in Japan, each exploring the maturation of a child protagonist who searches for something beyond himself or herself. In each case that search, which occurs for the most part on the level of the individual, is complemented by a societal search for meaning, as upheaval seems the omnipresent state of the world. This balance between societal conflict and conflict within the individual is a mark of Paterson's historical fiction, though not of her contemporary realism. This balance dominates the three novels set in Japan and the one in China; it also plays a central role in *Lyddie,* a work of historical fiction set in nineteenth-century New England written two decades after Paterson's first novel.

The Sign of the Chrysanthemum

The Sign of the Chrysanthemum (1973), Katherine Paterson's first novel, points toward the hard lessons she would push in subsequent novels—lessons about the harshness of life, about accepting that which, it seems, cannot be accepted. They are not lessons that lead to despair. Inevitably what Paterson's characters learn is that life is not art; it is not a child's novel where things are all tidily settled at the end. People do not go forth on adventures—whether in a schoolyard or in one's home or in the Molocca Islands—and then, like Dr. Dolittle, go quietly home to brewing tea and buttered biscuits. Yet, despite untidy endings, her characters hope.

The lessons Muna learns are of this type. Expressed implicitly in the novel, they lead inevitably to the novel's concluding line, which encapsulates all of what Muna learns. Perhaps Muna's most explicit lesson is that all mysteries are not solved, all questions are not resolved, and all strands of all stories are not neatly tied together. By the end of the novel Muna—and the reader—still does not know if the ronin (a renegade samurai) Takanobu is his father. It is possible, though the reader feels it to be unlikely, given Takanobu's varying stance toward Muna and Kiyomori's revelation that there are at least 200 samurai with the chrysanthemum tattoo. But the question remains open for Muna.

A correlating lesson Muna comes to accept—and that the reader, too, must learn willy-nilly—is that we do not need to know all parts of all stories. (One is reminded here of Aslan's frequent injunctions to the children of the *Narnia Chronicles* against trying to find out stories one does not need to know, or the fox in *The Hobbit* who never finds out why this party of dwarves and hobbits is tramping through the woods.) By the end of the novel Muna does not know what has happened to Takanobu, nor is he likely to find out. Akiko's story he knows only partially; he wonders if she brought the goldfish to the house on Rokujo Avenue. Of Fukuji's story—the loss of his wife and child—Muna knows nothing. The suggestion here is that all stories will not be finished or revealed.

Muna also learns the very hard lesson that there are dreadful things that happen that cannot be fixed. Not always, but sometimes. Muna can repair the evil he has done to himself by stealing Fukuji's sword, and he can end the destructive cycle he is on by breaking—though with difficulty—relations with Takanobu. But he cannot stop Akiko's being sold into prostitution any more than he can stop the battle between the Heiki and Genji clans in Kyoto, the ironically named Capital of Eternal Peace. In some things he is powerless.

This lesson, too, has a correlating lesson: pain and hurt are real and cannot be expunged by so-called happy endings. At the end of the novel Muna has found his place, but there is pain left. When he thinks about the name he would like to give himself, he recalls that his desire for a noble name "belonged to his daydream world of many months before, before Takanobu had reappeared and Kawaki had died. Before he had let go of his phantom of a father. Before he knew what happened to beautiful girls who were orphaned. Before he knew that he himself could lie and steal and betray."[1] These events will stay with Muna, despite his good situation at the end of the novel.

These are hard lessons, but Muna learns that the proper response to them is hope, not despair. "Hope is better than nothing" (53), Muna dreams of telling Takanobu as he continues his search for his father, and in fact Muna speaks more truly than he knows. There is a real possibility (which Kijomori suggests to Fukuji) that Muna's father can be identified. And as Muna becomes a swordsmith there is the possibility that he will be able to rescue Akiko—though this is held out as a slimmer hope. What is significant in his lessons is that Muna is, by the end of the novel, able to live with these hopes without being consumed and withered by the tasks they represent. Muna has learned that there are no quick and easy solutions; he can neither come to Kyoto and instantly find his father nor run to Rokujo Avenue and liberate Akiko. But he can wait and hope, in the meantime learning the lessons of who he himself is—lessons Fukuji will teach.

These lessons are nothing new to readers familiar with Katherine Paterson's novels: we recognize Jess, Gilly, Park, and Lyddie as descendents of Muna. For readers in 1973, however, the lessons Muna learned must have seemed hard, though embedded in an exciting tale of a boy searching for his father in the midst of an exciting city on the edge of an exciting rebellion. And of course they were hard.

Muna's story begins as a quest for his unknown father, though Muna will find that what he is actually searching for is himself. With the death of his mother, Muna feels free to leave the island on which he had been a serf and travel to Kyoto, where he hopes to find his father, a Heike warrior. He does not know that Kyoto is about to burst into civil war. Having stowed aboard a ship, Muna is befriended by the renegade samurai Takanobu, who promises to meet him in the city. Takanobu finds a job for Muna in the Imperial Stables, and though it quickly becomes evident that he is being used as a spy, Muna is filled with a sense of belonging and becomes deeply attached to the ronin.

When a fire erupts at a bar in which Takanobu has been drinking (a fire Takanobu may have started as part of the revolt against the Heike clan), Muna believes him to be dead and is overcome by smoke while trying to rescue him. Muna is rescued by Fukuji, the swordsmith. Impressed by Fukuji's self-discipline and art, and grateful for his kindness, Muna becomes his servant, and a strong bond grows between them. At the same time, Muna grows close to Akiko, who had shown kindness to him when he first came to Kyoto.

But these bonds are threatened when Takanobu returns, claims that he is Muna's father, and asks Muna to steal one of Fukuji's swords. Muna, angry and desperate after Akiko is sold into prostitution, agrees, but when he brings the sword and demands that Takanobu acknowledge their relationship openly, the ronin laughs. Muna runs away into the woods and buries the sword, now having lost Akiko, Takanobu, and Fukuji. He becomes a beggar, hiding from Fukuji, and only after many months, on the eve of the Genji revolt, is he able to bring himself to return the sword. He is more than surprised when Fukuji welcomes him back, accepts the returned sword, and allows him once again to serve. In time, as Muna comes to accept himself, Fukuji—who has in all senses but one become Muna's father—grants Muna the apprenticeship for which he had longed. And with it a home.

Perhaps because it was a first novel, *The Sign of the Chrysanthemum* did not attract the wide critical attention by reviewers that later Paterson novels were to garner. One British reviewer dismissed it curtly, calling it a story "in which the by-blow of a passing samurai has a picaresque walk on the wild side in search of his father."[2] Other reviewers were more accurate, however. The reviewer of *Publishers Weekly*—the review placed just over that of that year's Newbery winner, *The Slave Dancer*—praised the novel for its plot line: "How the boy resolves his problems and makes a new life is a question that will keep readers guessing and interested."[3] In *Horn Book* Virginia Haviland praised it for its characterization, citing "the confused but sometimes quick-witted boy; the philosophical, deeply kind master; and Takanobu, a renegade samurai warrior, now a completely amoral drifter who takes advantage of Muna's innocence."[4]

But two years after its publication, the novel received its most insightful review, appearing in the *Times Literary Supplement* under the unlikely title of "Feminine Insights": "The book is about pain, wisdom, choosing, and growing up, but it is far from didactic. The story is exciting, moving and unpredictable, and is presented with precision and economy of language."[5] This could be a review of most of Paterson's novels, which focus on the very edge of growing up, an edge that, to cross over, almost always involves pain. But the crux in Paterson's work is that the pain is part of the process of growth. As Virginia Haviland suggests in her review, at the end of the novel "the boy's search is fruitless and his dreams demolished, [but] Muna finds himself" (468). So, although I do not see the search as fruitless—Muna does indeed find a father, a spiritual father—certainly Haviland's conclusion is accurate: through the pain of growth and choice, Muna finds himself.

The novel is in fact more concerned with Muna's search for himself than for his father. It opens picturing Muna as a boy so devoted to a dream that is—most probably—a delusion that he cannot perform even the most meaningful ceremonies well. He is anxious to be done with his mother's funeral so that he can leave the island and his life as a serf and enter into the world of the samurai. The delusion is so strong that he is unable—and perhaps unwilling—to accurately assess the character of Takanobu. It is enough for Muna, whose Japanese name suggests his isolation from society, that he is included in a group. He does not question Takanobu's greeting of him when he appears at Rashomon Gate—"'Praise the devil!'" snorted the ronin and rolled over to sleep again" (23). He does not question the conspiratorial nature of the ronin's group, or their use of him as a spy in the Imperial Stables.

He does not question his desire to be allied to the ronin even after he perceives that Takanobu is a man with no honor. Holding the sword of Fukuji before him, Muna tries desperately to ensure that he would have a name, forcing Takanobu's allegiance: "'But if you are willing to be my father for the sale of this sword—then—then swear upon its blade that you will from this night regard me as your son. Swear—swear that I may follow you into battle or wherever fortune may lead you. Swear'—the boy's voice rose—'swear that you will give me the name of your family'" (93). It is as though Muna is repressing the knowledge that Takanodu has dishonored himself by selling his sword, that he has let Muna believe that he died at the Red Dog fire, that he has forced Muna into a terrible choice. For Muna, the need to belong overrides everything.

Takanobu's rejection of Muna—as inevitable and awful as something out of a Thomas Hardy novel—plunges Muna into what Paterson calls "the jaws of Hell" (128). And here the boy who began with such high dreams almost ends as a beggar—not because the dream was a bad one but because his vision of how that dream might be fulfilled, his understanding and vision of his father's identity, was so unrelentingly one-dimensional. To find a true father, he would first have to find himself. To do this, he must first get beyond the stultifying quest to belong at all costs. He must hope not just to find a biological father but a true father. Other Paterson characters—Gilly and Jimmy Jo among them—would find themselves on similar quests.

Though Takanobu is seen by Muna as the end of his quest, he is in reality its major blocking element. In the first encounter Takanobu might be perceived as rather gruff but essentially kind. He "pays" for Muna's passage and protects him from the ship's captain. But Takanobu is not the product of a kind world; he is the product of a world where, at the novel's end, "terror stalked avenue and alley" and "the victorious Heike routed Genji sympathizers from their hiding places and left their bodies unburied in the street" (127). It is a world where kindness unsupported by enormous strength is ineffectual, as Muna finds when his kindness to Akiko cannot prevent her degradation, or where Kawaki's kindness to Muna cannot forestall the sandalmaker's death.

Takanobu seems to have learned these lessons well. If the reader's first view of the ronin suggests that he is not the "completely amoral drifter" Virginia Haviland perceived, certainly by the end of the novel he has merited that description. When Muna seeks a commitment from Takanobu, his response is indicative of his character: "You little country fool! Do you think for one moment I would tie you about my neck like a great temple bell? . . . Dragging me down and clanging to my destruction?" (94). Takanobu is dramatic here; it is unlikely that Muna would contribute to his destruction. But what is significant here is that while Muna offers himself, Takanobu can respond out of nothing but expediency. Muna will no sooner run from him than Takanobu will attempt to betray him.

That attempted betrayal will bring together the man who claims to be Muna's father and the man who is Muna's father in all but biology. When Takanobu comes to Fukuji, offering to bring Muna to him if he is promised a sword as a reward, the two potential fathers are presented as polar opposites. Whereas Takanobu is gruff, rude, and imperious, Fukuji is proper. Where Takanobu is dishonorable, Fukuji is caring.[6]

Fukuji's concern is, from Takanobu's perspective, a weakness: "'You are steel, swordsmith. Tempered and polished—so polished. But'—he waved his finger toward the other's nose—'but I perceive a scratch'" (106). That scratch is Muna. Takanobu claims him as his son, but Fukuji uses the chrysanthemum tattoo—a damning sign that Takanobu was once allied to the clan he now fights against—to lead Takanobu to withdrawing his claim, if indeed it was ever valid. Takanobu flees, having been exposed, and Fukuji brings water to wash the courtyard of him, a blight on the secure and bound world of Fukuji.

It is this world Fukuji offers Muna—one marked by order, clarity, and precision. It is a world marked by patience—a quality Muna must learn. It is a world marked by acceptance of oneself—a state to which Muna must come. It is a world of peace, distinct from the quarrels of the city. And like the house of the sandalmaker, it is a world of kindness. After the battle in the Capital of Eternal Peace, Fukuji brings in the homeless and lays pallets in his rooms for the wounded and dying; he and Muna—who will share in these acts of kindness and who has himself been the recipient of Fukuji's kindness—sleep on the stone floor of the kitchen. Here Muna has come closer than ever to entering Fukuji's world.

The ballads Fukuji plays and sings are mirrors of his world: ordered, precise, artistic, peaceful.

> Has this world
> Been from ancient days
> Full of sorrow?
> Or has it become so
> For me alone? (61)

The songs Fukuji sings are reflections of his own life—here probably the death of his wife and child—but they are reflections ordered in tranquility. The sorrow has not lost its potency, but it is placed in a larger context through the medium of art that helps Fukuji to come to it in peace. That this song also reflects Muna's situation—he thinks of it when he realizes Kawaki is dying and Akiko will, like himself, be an orphan—suggests that he has the same kind of sensibilities that Fukuji holds.

The inner peace and self-control that these songs represent allow Fukuji to remain outside, though not aloof from, the squabbles that divide the Heike and Genji clans. He sings of the horrors that rivalry has caused:

> And my blood cries out to you, my son,
> The white banner is stained with scarlet.
> Turn and see, turn and see, the mighty
> house brought low. (51)

It is this song that leads Fukuji to one of his few moments of bitterness in this novel, where he condemns the pride of the two clans that has led to such suffering. And, typically, he sees in the agony of this specific situation a general principle: "Perhaps a man is never truly destroyed except by his own hand" (51).

It is this principle Muna seems about to illustrate. From the beginning of the novel Muna is fiercely proud of his Heike background; it is what prompts him to leave his island. His pride—and his hope—will make him overlook Takanobu's dishonorable ways, will make him resentful of the "woman's work" he performs for Fukuji, will make him unable to return the stolen sword to Fukuji. It is only when he becomes a beggar, chased and betrayed, that he can overcome his pride and return to Fukuji. And there he finds what is least expected, what perhaps even another prodigal son could not allow himself to hope for: forgiveness.

So Muna returns to Fukuji's house, and there he finds an end to his two quests. He finds his true father, whom he had almost rejected, and he finds his name: "For several days he thought again about his name—the one he would carry and give to his children. He took out and examined again all the grand names he had once considered, but now they seemed pompous and unsuitable. He was what he was. No other name would change that" (130). Muna has found himself.

It is a hard finding, mirrored by his recollections of the sturdy and seemingly secure tree on his home island, "his place for sorrow and anger and dreams" (42). Here he would fantasize about his noble father and close his ears to the cries of his searching mother. But after he flees from Takanobu, he dreams of himself under the tree as it is ripped away by a storm, exposing him to the fierce sneers of Takanobu. In the whirlwind of the city, Muna has delusions shattered, leaving him exposed.

His exposure, however, is a healing experience. Fukuji teaches Muna that to come to terms with your life, you must know yourself fully. Only then can you separate and discard the things you seem to want from the deeper yearnings for the things you truly need: a family, a home, an acceptance of oneself—none of which Takanobu can provide. "What do you think of yourself?" Fukuji counters when Muna demands to know what Fukuji thinks of him. "If you are not content with yourself, what does it matter what I think?" (80). Muna learns Fukuji's lessons only after great hardship, reflected in the inscription of the chrysanthemum-sheathed sword that Fukuji gives him, the very last line of the novel: "Through fire is the spirit forged" (132). And having learned this lesson, Muna becomes Fukuji's apprentice.

The apprenticeship is the gleam of hope that peers dimly out of the troubled world of *The Sign of the Chrysanthemum,* as gleams will peer out through many troubled worlds in Paterson's work. Just beneath the story of Muna is the conflict between the Taira and Minamoto families, the Heike and Genji clans. This conflict, which resulted in years of civil war in twelfth-century Japan, erupts fully into the action of Muna's story only at the conclusion of the novel, but its unremitting horror is a dreadful balance of the fulfillment of Muna's hopes. That the Heike clan is victorious in the battle Muna experiences is tainted by the fact that the Heike clan would eventually be defeated with the death of the seven-year-old emperor in the sea battle of Dannovra. But this is outside the confines of this novel. In the end, Muna has been swayed by hope—a hope that, though unlikely at times, will be shared by many of Paterson's characters.

Of Nightingales That Weep

Only a year after the publication of *The Sign of the Chrysanthemum* Paterson finished *Of Nightingales That Weep* (1974), a longer and in some ways fuller work. Paterson set both novels in medieval Japan, both during the conflict between the Heike and Genji clans. This second novel is set late in the period, so that while the first depicts a Heike victory, the second depicts the ultimate fall of the Heike clan. In both novels the characters live with the swirl of political events, though it is Takiko who is most affected.

The two novels are cousins in more than their historical time, however. Both protagonists, Muna and Takiko, are young adolescents at the beginning of the narratives, propelled into maturity willy-nilly. Both are the children of a samurai warrior, intensely aware of the social codes that such parentage entails. Both must deal with the loss of parents; both search for a father, though Takiko's search takes on quite a different form. Both search for a real home, though Takiko's search takes the form of searching for something she already has. Like Muna, she has made choices that alienate her from that home.

In *Of Nightingales That Weep* the most parental figure—Goro—is again an artisan. He allows the theme of hope to resound in this novel, as Fukuji had done in *The Sign of the Chrysanthemum.* Like Fukuji, he is a silent character, above political conflicts, who practices his craft with grace, dignity, and excellence. In the end he has experienced more hurt even than Takiko; it seems that he, like Takiko, is about to abandon all hope. (One thinks here of Fukuji's despair at the loss of Muna.) But in the end, though the hurt is real, the healing is real, too, and a home—like that of Fukuji and Muna—is established.

Some of the differences in the novels stem from Paterson's integration of the private world of Takiko with the public world of the Heike-Genji conflict. In many ways Takiko is defined by accepted social codes—and accepted political ones as well. These codes are certainly called into question insofar as they intrude into family life (one such code leads Takiko to almost commit suicide), but they gird Takiko closely, and her decisions are formed by them. Muna is not so closely bound. It is this greater integration of private and public worlds that brings such codes to the fore in the later novel.

A second significant difference—and one that points to Paterson's growth as a novelist—is the larger cast of characters and their greater psychological depth in *Of Nightingales That Weep.* Whereas *The Sign of the Chrysanthemum* focuses on three characters (Muna, Takanobu, and Fukuji), the second novel juggles an enormous cast. They may be divided along the lines of the private and public worlds, though they are connected by Takiko. Takiko, her mother, Goro, Ichiro, and Fusa represent the family grouping; Takiko, Lady Kiyomori, the little emperor, and Mieko form the court grouping. These groupings represent two different worlds. The first is principally concerned with the private world, and here the characters face the difficulties family tensions establish. The second focuses on the public tensions—tensions that destroy little children and threaten women with physical attacks.

It is a large cast, and the characters are often paired: Goro is set against Takiko's samurai father, her mother against Lady Kiyomori, Ichiro against the emperor. While Takiko can straddle the two worlds for a time, no one else can, particularly her presumed lover, Hideo. Even she must ultimately make a choice between worlds. The minor characters, too, are developed: the confident Meiko, who at the end seems to have a greater sense of honor and protocol than Takiko; Fusa, an ancestor of Trotter in *The Great Gilly Hopkins;* Munemori, the defeated general who mixes despair with dignity. Though the novel may at times strain with such a large cast, it is no small measure of its success that all the characters are balanced so well—delicately, but well.

The story opens as Takiko, her hair being brushed, learns that her father is going to fight for the Heike cause. His death plunges the family into poverty—as well as danger from the victorious Genji clan. Soon Takiko's mother decides to marry Goro, the potter. But when Takiko sees him, she is terrified by his ugliness, and he is hurt by her repulsion. Yet gradually they come to peace as Takiko plays her koto, charming her parents and eventually Ichiron, her new stepbrother.

Takiko's musical skill and beauty lead to her becoming a court servant for Princess Aoi. When she plays before the child emperor, he is so pleased by her performance that she is asked to become part of the imperial court. She accepts, bringing with her her servant and confidant, Meiko. But the political situation turns against the court, and Takiko accompanies the emperor and his train as they flee from the coming Genji forces. Though the imperial court is infiltrated by a Genji spy—Hideo, with whom Takiko falls in love—they are relatively secure.

It is during this period that Goro comes to request that Takiko return to help her mother, who is again pregnant. Takiko refuses, ostensibly because of her duty to the emperor, but principally because of her hope of seeing Hideo again. Angered, Goro returns and asks Fusa, an elderly nurse whom he had been forced to send back to her village because of Genji ravages, to come back. She returns, bringing with her the plague that kills Goro's wife and son. Blaming Takiko, Goro resigns himself to a life of loneliness and despair.

Encouraged by Genji dissension, General Munemori decides on a bold plan to return to the mainland and reassert the dominance of the imperial court. But in the ensuing sea battle, forces unexpectedly turn against the Heike clan. In a dreadful kind of honorable despair, the ladies of the court throw themselves, together with the young emperor, into the sea; most drown. Some, together with Takiko, are taken alive. Takiko, filled with guilt and shame at not following the court but hopeful of seeing Hideo again, is indeed rescued by her lover, and she returns to Goro.

She is, of course, quite surprised at what she finds. Goro is enormously resentful, and many months pass before their work in the fields together—and the music of the koto—begin to break down the barriers of mutual anger and hostility. Little by little, Takiko loses much of the delicate polish and beauty of the court, so that when Hideo finally comes for her after Takiko has spent anxious weeks looking down the road, he is repelled by her, particularly by a scar she has acquired. They lapse into clichéd courtesy, and Takiko bids him farewell. She resolves to enter a convent with other ladies at the court, but once there she discovers her true calling to heal. She returns to a now-despondent Goro, and the novel ends with the celebration of their marriage and the birth of a daughter. The last line of the novel suggests the nature of their new life, full of hope and remembered pain: "Then they laughed and wept together without caring if the peasants outside the hut were listening or not."[7]

The focus here is all on Takiko. Though the complexity of the political events in this novel is greater than that of *The Sign of the Chrysanthemum,* leading to many more than the one passage in the first novel dedicated to a narrative of the Heike-Genji struggle, the reader is almost constantly focused on Takiko. Presented as a spiritual cousin of Muna, she, too, is torn by loyalties; loyal to the Heike clan, she is attracted to a Genji spy; loyal to the court, she hears the call of her family. Like Muna, she makes decisions based on immediately perceived needs; she will not betray Hideo, despite the lack of commitment on his part. She will ignore the needs of her family, rationalizing her actions as a call to duty, for the sake of a possible meeting with Hideo, much as Muna will make the rash decision to steal Fukuji's sword to force Takanobu into a commitment.

In fact, over and again Takiko seems to make the wrong decisions. Her initial decision to go to the court of Princess Aoi seems to come not out of her desire to have a family but out of her need to be at the center of things—perhaps even to be admired. There she finds herself in a place where sexual exploitation is a real, imminent danger. She rejects Goro as Muna rejects Fukuji, but her basis is merely physical; he is an ugly man. She fails, at least at first, to perceive his hurt, his isolation, and his astonishing capacity for love and forgiveness. Her allegiance to Hideo comes out of a kind of blindness, an infatuation that does not allow her to see how he uses her in his spying, how he is attracted only to her beauty, how he never returns—and clearly never holds—the kind of allegiance she offers. Her decision to not return with Goro to help her mother lends indirectly to the death of two people whom she loves and leaves her in the situation where she must commit suicide or be captured by the Genji. Her decision to enter the convent seems to be a final rejection of Goro's needs.

And yet despite all this Takiko is called a healer:

> "I have been thinking," the Empress continued, "about our nation. It lies wounded, Takiko. Perhaps the wound is mortal. I pray not. But where do we turn for healing? . . . Do you remember how my mother used to say that your music was better for my son than medicine? Perhaps, Takiko, we are meant to learn that beauty can heal. . . . If your music had healing power when you were a vain and thoughtless child, what might it accomplish now?" (167–68)

This is what propels Takiko to return to Goro, and this is the redemptive beauty of this novel: Takiko, despite all her bad decisions, heals. The doll at the novel's opening who is kneeling and complaining because the servant combing her hair pulls too hard becomes the woman in the conclusion crying out in triumph at childbirth and establishing a true home with one who loves her—and who is loved in turn.

Though Muna, too, is in one sense a healer—he will heal the aching loneliness of Fukuji—Takiko's gift of healing is tied to her singing and her koto. It is the instrument Takiko hides from danger, wraps lovingly, and plays. It is, after all, her music that engages the court, that soothes the emperor, that draws her family together, and that helps to reconcile her with Goro. Even when the physical beauty that had caused such a sensation at court was gone, there was still the music, the deeper gift. It is that gift—a gift that brought people into almost literal harmony with each other—that stands opposed to the discord of the political strife.

Perhaps, ironically, the music, represented by the koto of Goro's family, is the one element of Goro's world that Takiko brings with her to court. Goro's world is that of art honestly crafted, of hard outside work, of good sleep after labor well performed, of comradeship, of commitments. For the most part, the world of the court is almost exactly opposed to it—it is a world of political and sexual intrigue, which Takiko's music propels not to companionship but to rape. It is a world of leisure, of ill-health. It is a world suffocatingly controlled by ceremony, a kind of ceremony that is so deadening that it steals childhood. It is a world with a literally fatal sense of tradition that kills a seven-year-old boy—a boy who was never allowed to be a child.

Takiko is seduced (literally) by the world of the court. Though there is clearly some good there—her friendship with Meiko, her growing love of the child emperor, her admiration for some ladies of the court who have weathered enormous hardships—this is clearly not her true home. She will not recognize this until Hideo's rejection of her—a rejection that suggests more than anything else the superficiality of the courtly world. Takiko has fallen into this superficiality, rejecting Goro and becoming infatuated with Hideo, both on the basis of mere physical appearance.

And it is here that the odd pot that Goro has made takes on so much of its significance:

> She had never seen such a misshapen vessel. Goro despised absolute symmetry, she knew. But this strange cup looked as though the potter had tried to wring it like a piece of laundry. Even the lid was a grotesque fit. And the brilliant black glaze had been smeared on haphazardly so that the grays and yellows of the original clay broke through. What had Goro been thinking of? . . . She lifted the lid and gasped. The underside of the lid had been painstakingly gold-leafed. Etched in the gold was a delicate painting of a bird in flight—perhaps a nightingale. (147–48)

Though it seems to be an ill-made cup, Kamaji the merchant has placed it with his finest pieces. Later, it is offered as a gift to Buddha, and when the empress, now a nun, examines its outside, Takiko assures her it is quite beautiful inside. The reply is telling: "It is not possible that the inside could be lovelier than this" (166). Takiko's first rejection of it comes on an impulse as quick and unthinking as that which led to her rejection of Goro and her attraction to Hideo. But the empress sees something else: the grays and yellows of the original clay, the substance that gives the pot its true beauty.

The interior of the pot reinforces this meaning. The gilt inside, painstakingly applied and etched, is most unexpected, and perhaps breathtaking because of that. It is a meaning that applies first to Goro but then later to Takiko. Both come to have outsides that seem unpleasant, but both come to know themselves beyond that outside, and to know each other. That is why the last scene is so full of redemptive glory: they know each other deeply, and in knowing they love. Whereas before Takiko had been ready to let herself be swallowed by a convent and Goro had sat for three days waiting for the plague until he realized that he had been "condemned to life" (122), at the end of the novel the birth of their child signals their new life.

And so Takiko becomes a prototypical Paterson character. She begins in growing turmoil, affected by her own superficiality, which allows her to rationalize the dismissal of her family commitments. She refuses to accept the love offered by Goro and even by the matronly Fusa: "She would not be seduced by kindness. This woman was part of the terrible household here. She maintained her stony silence" (20). Takiko refuses to look deeply, beyond the surface, past her own resentments. But she—like Gilly, Park, and Jimmy Jo—will learn the lessons that lead to the establishment of a home.

And herein lies the terrible irony of Paterson's integration of the public and private worlds. As one public family—the Heike—is destroyed and another beset by internal rivalries—the Genji—the private family of Goro and Takiko is remade, like that of Wang Lee and Mei Lin in *Rebels of the Heavenly Kingdom.* In the midst of a world at war, there is this small hut where joy and family abide. Takiko's long-held hope has been fulfilled in a way that not she, Goro, or the reader could have imagined.

The Master Puppeteer

With *The Master Puppeteer* (1975) Paterson changes her setting in terms of time, though not place. The story occurs in eighteenth-century Osaka, and though removed by several centuries from the Heiki-Genji conflict, the events are not unfamiliar. Once again the story of an individual—the young apprentice Jiro—is set against the backdrop of a society at war with itself. It is a city besieged. On the one hand there are the wealthy—those who control the supplies, who are protected by the guardians of the supplies: the police. Against these are set the street rovers who roam, destroy, and loot, partly to survive the famine and partly to destroy the possessions of the powerful, thereby hurting that unreachable class, at least obliquely.

In a society at war with itself, right relations seem almost irrelevant, yet *The Master Puppeteer* is a story about relations—relations that begin in disarray and move toward wholeness. It is a story of obligations and their cost, of how one goes about choosing which obligations to fulfill, of how one deals with mutually conflicting obligations. Should Hansi support his family or commit himself to the Robin Hood–like Saburo? Should Kinshi support his father, Yoshida, or work toward the support of the poor? Should Jiro support Okada at the cost of his allegiance to Kinshi? Should Jiro remain at the Hanaza, the puppet theater, being well-fed while his mother starves? These questions torment Jiro—and in some ways the reader—throughout the novel.

The story opens in the home of Hanji and Isako, expert puppet makers for the master puppeteer, Yoshida. They survive by making puppets, although their son, Jiro, seems clumsy and unable to help. When Hanji and Jiro deliver a puppet, Jiro is entranced by the world of the Hanaza, a world in which there seems to be plenty of food. When Yoshida suggests that Jiro be apprenticed to the theater, Hanji demurs, but Jiro's heart leaps. In fact, it is not long before Jiro runs away to join the theater, bringing with him the terrible knowledge that his father is gravely ill and his mother has cursed the day he was born for his desertion.

At the theater he becomes part of the group of young apprentices, where his abilities, though rough at first, bring him the affection of Yoshida Kinshi, the head boy and the son of the master puppeteer. His skills grow considerably, and soon he is performing in front of audiences, with the grudging acceptance of Yoshida. But outside the Hanaza things are growing worse. Jiro's father has gone away from the city, perhaps dying. Isako, his mother, has returned to become part of the night rovers. One night these rovers attack the theater and are kept out by its stout gate; Jiro hears his mother's voice crying out for food, and he does not open the gate to her.

During this time the clever thief Saburo is raiding the wealthy, simultaneously subsidizing the theater and supporting the poor with his exploits. Yet though he is supposed to be giving rice and goods to the poor, we never hear of any specific instance of this in the novel, suggesting that the poor affirm him principally for his ability to deceive the wealthy. Jiro's mother claims that if she knew who he was, she would betray him for a few days of rice.

Jiro believes he has discovered Saburo's identity. After his single trip home to see his mother and bring her food, he is attacked by a rogue samurai. Yoshida suddenly appears to rescue him, though he warns Jiro harshly not to reveal that they had ever met. While in Yoshida's house, stealing a script for the apprentices to memorize, Jiro comes across a basket used in one of Saburo's exploits. And in the theater's storehouse, he finds a sword he knows Saburo has stolen.

Convinced that Yoshida is Saburo, Jiro goes to the blind Okada, the oldest and most respected master in the theater, to ask him to convince Yoshida to help the night rovers. Here Jiro is concerned about his mother, but he is also fearful for Kinshi, who steals out at night to help the rovers, convinced that the small, single exploits of Saburo are useless. But when Jiro goes up to the storeroom to find the sword—the evidence that Okada asks for—he is confronted by Saburo himself, who is not Yoshida but Okada, the blind master. Okada is not convinced that Jiro is trustworthy, and fearfully Jiro runs away to find Isako and Kinshi on his own.

The city is in an uproar: the streets are filled with people, looting is rampant, buildings have been set ablaze, the police and firemen have been attacked by the crowds. Jiro meets his father and finds that the illness has been a pose; well-fed and comfortable, he has been faithful to Saburo. Jiro leaves him to find Isako and Kinshi (who has gone in search of Isako), and, posing as a fireman, he rescues them from the police; they had been arrested together. In fact, Kinshi had rescued Isako from becoming part of a looting mob, while she had rescued him when a policeman had sliced off his hand, believing him to be a looter. Jiro gets them both back to the theater, using a ruse not unlike that of Saburo.

At the theater right relations are restored. Yoshida recognizes his son's bravery and merit, though he seems unable to articulate this recognition. Okada recognizes that Jiro's loyalty to Kinshi and Yoshida, if not to him, is yet to be trusted. Isako has accepted the love and help of her son, and Jiro recognizes his obligations to her. The novel closes with Kinshi's comic remark that it is a mother's happiness to worry about her son, with comedy overlaying the serious point: Jiro, and in some ways Kinshi as well, has established the right relationship with his mother. His father, however, having abandoned his family, is not brought into the union.

Like the cities of *The Sign of the Chrysanthemum* and *Of Nightingales That Weep,* the city of Osaka in *The Master Puppeteer* is a city in turmoil, that outer setting thus reflecting the inner turmoil of Jiro. On the one hand Osaka is a city in the midst of crisis: food supplies are low and are being exploited by rich merchants, the police and firemen are losing control, and roving bands of the poor loot out of anger but also in a desperate attempt to survive. On the other hand, however, there is the Hanaza, which seems blissfully above the concerns. Here is the world of the imagination, of excellence in art and crafts, of plenty. There is no starvation here.

The conflicts in the novel come when these two worlds are bridged. Saburo provides such bridging; Okada is a master puppeteer in several senses. Yoshida, Okada's agent, is another bridge. And even Yoshida Kinshi is a bridge, as he steals out each night to help those roaming the streets, who themselves become such a bridge when they attack the Hanaza. Certainly the authorities observe this connection, closing down a play written by Okada that seems to represent too closely the cunning antics of Saburo, whom the police see as even more dangerous than "a stray Christian or two."[8]

Certainly the most significant bridge between these two worlds, though, is Jiro, and it is precisely this role that causes him such turmoil. Drawn by his imagination—and belly—to the theater, he is nevertheless drawn by ties of family obligation—and guilt—to his home. When Yoshida suggests a possible apprenticeship, Jiro is almost immediately besieged by conflicting loyalties:

> He didn't want to leave home, not because he was particularly happy, but because it was familiar and his father was usually kind. But he had been so hungry, and here at the theater they had food. . . . The theater would be an exciting life. . . . But there was Yoshida with his thin bamboo rod—what happened to clumsy apprentices?. . . And yet, perhaps if he came to the theater, he would stop being clumsy. Maybe clumsiness went with being hungry and having made your mother unhappy by being born. (16)

Believing that one is the cause of one's mother's unhappiness is a terrible burden, perhaps made worse because in this case it is true. Both mother and child must deal with that burden before the novel is over.

Jiro is drawn to the world of the puppet theater at first sight. This world so consumes him, calls so much of his attention, that, although he occasionally feels guilt and shame over his family's situation, he acts for that family only haphazardly—behavior that is also redeemed by the end of the novel. For much of the novel the puppet theater is the real and immediate world for Jiro; even the plays take on a higher reality: "Jiro soon forgot the presence of the men. They became far less real than the dolls, whose tragedy was being played out as Okada's magic voice spun a web of dread about his audience" (27). In focusing on his art, Jiro forgets the other tragedies being played out beyond the walls of the Hanaza. Like Takiko—but unlike Fukuji—Jiro seems to use his art to insulate himself from the reality.

From Jiro's point of view, he has gone to the theater so that he will not burden his parents. In fact, he thinks he may be able to earn money to help them—a belief that is partly true, partly a rationalization. From his mother's point of view, Jiro has abandoned his home when his father is ill and there is no money in the house so that he might live comfortably. This, too, is partly true and partly muddled by her own desperation. Their perceptions so at odds, Isako pronounces what Jiro has always feared she believed: she curses the day he was born. And Jiro, fearing rejection, does not obey his first impulse to rush to her and throw his arms about her; instead he returns to the theater—thus, in Isako's mind, confirming her opinion.

Jiro is not the only one to abandon Isako. Hanji deserts her as well through deception in order to join Saburo and be well fed. (Had this novel been written from Isako's perspective, the story might have been almost too painful, for Isako seems to lack the tenacity and strength that allows a character like Paterson's Lyddie to survive equally dreadful realizations.) Hanji does not seem much burdened by his desertion, but certainly Jiro, hurt by his mother's curse, is also burdened by guilt over his situation as opposed to hers. Why should he be sated while she starves? Why should he not support her while his father is ill? What would have happened had she, with other night rovers, broken in to the Hanaza while he was wielding a club to keep the rioters out? Why should it be Kinshi, rather than Jiro himself, who goes out into the night to find Isako and rescue her from the night rovers?

Though Jiro cannot bear to answer the first question, he must answer the last, especially after Kinshi seems to have disappeared. And so Jiro goes out to find them, even as he is convinced the Saburo is out to silence him. In a city gone mad, blazing with fires, he is found by his father, who has been sent out by Saburo. Hanji is not searching for Isako, and Jiro soon abandons him, perhaps explaining why Hanji is not in the renewed—and enlarged—

family circle at the end of the novel. When Isako first sees him, she cries, "It's my boy! He's come to get me!" (163). He has indeed: the curse is lifted, and right relations are restored.

At the beginning of Jiro's apprenticeship, Kinshi tells the younger boy that "we all learn here . . . by the honorable path of horrible mistakes" (41). Here Kinshi is describing how one learns to manipulate a puppet, but in fact this is a line that could be used to describe many of Paterson's characters, particularly Jiro. He learns through the honorable path of error. When he is first brought into the theater, he is anxious that his father come to see him, but he himself neglects attending to his father when he believes Hanji to be ill. During his one visit to his mother he makes no provisions for her, offering her food for one day only, holding back from searching out and fulfilling deeper needs. When Isako calls from outside the walls of the Hanaza, he does not go to her. These are not the acts of a callous child, however; Jiro yearns to be the dutiful son he believes he is not. In the end, having learned the significance of loyalties from his association with Kinshi, he will have grown in that direction.

After the night raid against the Hanaza, Jiro does determine to help Isako. "I'll find some way to help you. I swear it. I will" (113), he pleads to himself, and though he has as yet no idea how he will do this, he is determined. Later he decides to go with Kinshi to help the poor, particularly his mother. But Kinshi is not yet ready to allow Jiro to put himself in danger. After Kinshi slips out that night, "Jiro turned over and over, banging his head each time against the hard pillow as though to knock away the sound of his mother's voice and the vision of her pinched and hungry face" (120).

Only at the end of the novel does Jiro, drawn inevitably by his loyalties, go to rescue Kinshi and Isako. And only after that rescue can he admit to her—and to himself—that both he and his father had deserted her. It is a charge Isako does not deny. Yoshida later tells Jiro that "a man must pay a terrible price to maintain his oath" (175–76), but Jiro has come to realize that there are some prices too high to pay. Perhaps even Yoshida comes to realize this, as he allows Isako to live at the Hanaza.

In the end right relationships are established—or reestablished. Kinshi has earned the grudging love and even admiration of his father, though one doubts that Yoshida's love will ever be expressed openly. Jiro and Kinshi have established mutual bonds of loyalty. Jiro and Yoshida have met, for a brief moment, as absolute equals recognizing that some loyalties are perhaps more significant than others. (It is a recognition also shared by Okada.) And Jiro and Isako have reunited.

None of these right relationships has been established easily. Each involves pain and, in some measure, a repudiation of the past, though its effects are still apparent. For Kinshi, the price has been a lost hand. For Yoshida, the price has been dashed hopes. For Jiro, the price is the recognition of his own honorable path of horrible mistakes. But the relations are established nonetheless.

Rebels of the Heavenly Kingdom

Half a dozen books were to pass before Paterson turned once again to the east to write her fourth work of historical fiction, *Rebels of the Heavenly Kingdom* (1983). It was a difficult writing for Paterson, because it was a difficult period in China's history: "There were times, notably the winter of 1982, when I wanted more than anything to give up. History is so cruel, and I am repelled by violence. But I kept on, not simply because my passion for the story drove me on, but because all about me I could see the leaders of my own country, both political and religious, justifying violence and injustice as a means to peace. It lent an urgency to the writing."[9] This is indeed a story of a search for peace, both for a society and an individual. But it is also the story of that search gone wrong.

Rebels of the Heavenly Kingdom marks a departure from Paterson's first three works in terms of setting: the action is placed in mid-nineteenth-century China rather than medieval Japan. But the major themes she had begun to explore in the earlier novels—the nature of the family, the redeeming power of hope—are explored in perhaps even greater depth in *Rebels of the Heavenly Kingdom*:

> Here were people who were saying that to harm or kill a fellow creature was against God's law. They were opposed to any sort of oppression—foot-binding, prostitution, multiple marriages, the buying and selling of human beings for any purpose. They did not kill, steal, use alcohol or opium, or bow to any graven image. Moreover, they believed that every child had a right to an education, regardless of sex or parentage. All this at a time when in America we were still arguing about whether or not God meant us to hold slaves. I was fascinated by these people. Where had they gotten their high ideals, and what had become of them? And I was led into the tragic story of what happens when persons of high ideals take them into a holy crusade to save the world.[10]

This is in some ways a novel about a movement, but it is also about individuals. Again Paterson balances public and private worlds. Both Wang Lee and Mei Lin are protagonists who seem to find precisely what they had hoped for in the public world and who then discover the utter corruption of that hope, both in those they had trusted in the Taiping movement and, perhaps more important, in themselves as well.

While Wang Lee is working in his parents' field, he is abducted by bandits who force him to carry away their loot from his own house. (It is the time of the Taiping Rebellion against the Manchu dynasty, and many renegade soldiers have turned to banditry.) Wang Lee is forced to work for the bandits, until one day he is bought by a mysterious "gentleman" who then frees him. His savior is actually Mei Lin, a girl with unbound feet who is part of the Taiping Rebellion. Wang Lee tentatively joins the group, and Mei Lin teaches him the philosophical tenets of the Taiping, a mixture of Confucianism and Christianity with a stress on the nature of community.

Accompanied by an older rebel, Chu, Mei Lin brings Wang Lee up into the mountains and to the Taiping community. At first Wang Lee is confused and wary of the group. Their rejection of Chinese tradition—for example, breaking and binding the feet of young girls—and their leveling of societal distinctions cause him to question. But Mei Lin's stories of Feng, the spiritual leader of the Taiping, the community's emphasis on hope and peace, the way in which everyone in the community shares with everyone else—all this leads Wang Lee toward accepting his new friends.

Early on, however, the community's commitment to peace and to the preservation of life is tested: Feng and Hung, two of the most significant of the Taiping lenders, are held under guard by imperial Manchu troops. Yang, one of the several kings of the Taiping, organizes the attack that will free them, and three battles rapidly follow. At the battle of Chin-t'ien they are freed, and the leaders of the Taiping seem unaware of the irony of the presence of bloodied corpses juxtaposed with a hymn praising the sanctity of life and the Great Peace. Instead, the leaders of the rebellion see themselves as having taken over the dynastic mantle, and Hung is proclaimed the first king of the new dynasty.

The rest of the political story of this novel is a working out of these early steps to the final act against any pretense of a Great Peace: Hung's assassination of Yang and his family because they were growing to be a threat to his own reign. Wang Lee is caught up in these events as they develop. Having been baptized into the community, he now finds a new identity: no longer a peasant, he is destined to be part of the dynasty that will overthrow the Manchu government and come to rule the world.

Wang Lee learns to kill, as imperial raiders come against the Taiping mountain camps. At first difficult, the task becomes almost meaningless after a time, done virtually without thought. As the Taiping grow stronger and the imperial troops are weakened by dissension, the rebels come down from the mountains to attack government-held cities. Wang Lee is promoted, and soon he hardly even smells the blood he spills in the course of the series of successful battles that the Taiping wage.

Mei Lin has not yet begun to doubt the direction the rebellion is taking, but she has felt, almost unconsciously, some qualms. So that the soldiers' hearts would remain with a single purpose, the camp has been divided into male and female sides. Families are divided, and Mei Lin senses but cannot articulate the problems with this. She is also now separated from Wang Lee, so the two cannot openly acknowledge, even to thenselves, the relationship that is developing between them. She takes solace in giving all of her attention to her role as one of the horsewomen of God, serving under San-niang, the sister of one of the kings. Mei Lin learns archery and horseback riding, and soon she is one of the elite warriors.

Wang Lee has remained separated from Mei Lin, though he, too, has begun to sense the oddity of such a separation. He has also begun to tutor Shen, a scholar and teacher himself who has come to learn the Taiping principles. Shen has saved Wang Lee from death, and they become close friends. But soon Shen begins to ask disturbing questions about Taiping doctrine, and soon he begins to point out inconsistencies in behavior: How can the Taiping rulers, who preach the sanctity of life, indulge in so much killing? And how can they demand obedience to arbitrary laws that cause so much pain? And how can they explain their own tyranny? Wang Lee cannot answer these questions and resorts to rote declarations. Eventually Wang Lee denounces him secretly, and Yang has Shen executed. It is the most dishonorable deed Wang Lee has performed up to this time; when Chu fears for him because of his association with Shen, Wang replies that he is not a traitor, but his conscience suggests that he is, and he dreams of Shen's head on a pike.

When the Taiping take the city of Chuan-chou, they conduct a dreadful massacre. Wang Lee kills arbitrarily, even the elderly and the beggars. But he is caught up sharply when, after beheading a woman who has tried to stop him from entering her house, Wang Lee shoots and kills a two-year-old child. The horror of it comes on him, and he is eventually found by Chu and Mei Lin at the river, trying to wash himself clean. He tries to articulate what he has discovered to Mei Lin, but she will not allow herself to listen. Later, after she has escaped death during an ambush, Wang Lee finally tells Mei Lin of his love, but again she will not listen. She remains committed to the precepts of the Taiping, refusing to acknowledge openly their tyranny. Even when one of the kings orders the execution of his own parents, Mei Lin, who knows that this is against Feng's teachings, cannot break from the movement.

Neither can Wang Lee. He is recruited to become a spy in the city the Taiping hope to take next: Changsha. On the way, he stops to see the house of his parents. They are gone, but the bandits who caught him are not; they capture him, bring him to the city, and sell him as a female slave—he will bring more money that way. Here he is caught behind the lines and feels stymied as Mei Lin continues to collect honors. (Wang Lee does not know that Mei Lin has begun to receive love letters from Hung himself, against all the laws of the Taiping, and that Mei Lin has had to face, though not acknowledge, some of the faithlessness of the Taiping rulers.) Wang Lee befriends the young daughter of the household to which he had been sold; he is horrified by the breaking of her feet, and to compensate he begins to teach her to read and write. But this rejection of tradition—which had once so horrified him—marks him as a rebel. He flees the city and begins his journey to find Mei Lin, for the army has bypassed Changsha and headed for Nanking. He follows the blood and destruction the army has left behind.

By now even San-niang has realized the horror of the Taiping Rebellion. When Nanking is taken and the dead are impossible to count, she sits on the walls and weeps. Wang Lee does not see this, for he reaches Nanking only after many days of walking. There he searches out Mei Lin, who is now betrothed to Hung, and they finally acknowledge their love. But the next morning the bride is gone, and when Wang Lee moves to stop her and bid farewell, he is knocked unconscious by Chu. He is dressed in women's clothes and carried out of the city as Chu's bride. Only outside the city does he find out that San-niang has taken Mei Lin's place and that Mei Lin has been one of his bearers.

The three don peasant clothes and return to the hut of Wang Lee's parents. The house is abandoned and wrecked, the fields all a-tangle, but the three work to repair the home and clear the ground, and they find the rice seed hidden by Wang Lee's parents. They plant, and they hope for new life.

If this summary seems inordinately long and complicated, it suggests the length and complexity of the novel. *Rebels of the Heavenly Kingdom* is almost double the length of some of Paterson's earlier works. The panorama of history that the characters move through is much more complex. And here Paterson deals with two characters who move on parallel journeys to the same point. In addition, Paterson is depicting the public world of the Taiping at the same time she depicts the private world of Wang Lee and Mei Lin, the public world defining much of the nature of the private world—at least for a time.

The novel's title is an expression of one of the principal tensions of the novel: the notion of rebellion. In one sense the rebellion preached by Feng and embraced particularly by Mei Lin is a spiritual rebellion, a discarding of the old traditions for a new enlightenment based on Christian principles. And yet this is also a political rebellion. Certainly this is the way that the Manchu forces see the movement—as a rebellion against the authorities. At first Hung and his followers seem to see the former element to be dominant, but as the novel progresses it is clear that the drive is toward a political domination, at the expense of the principial themes of the movement. In part this is symbolized by Feng's subordinate position to the other, more politically minded kings. But in an even greater sense it is suggested by the blending of motives and methods of the Taiping and imperial armies. As the peasants observe, in the end there is no distinction between them.

The title then becomes ambiguous, for the Taiping are rebels in at least two senses. Certainly they rebel against the Manchu dynasty. But as the novel progresses they also rebel against the principles of their Heavenly Kingdom, particularly that teaching which suggests that, although it cost an empire, one should not take a human life. This teaching sounds more and more ironically on the journey to Nanking, blending with the hymns of peace sung before the carnage of ruined cities.

The dual sense of rebellion is also mirrored in Wang Lee. While Mei Lin seems single-minded in pursuit of the principles of the Heavenly Kingdom, turning against the Taiping only when the movement turns against its own teachings, Wang Lee goes through various stages of rebellion. At first he resists but then embraces the teachings of the movement, becoming the unthinking fanatic who rejects disloyal thoughts. But in the end he—and

Mei Lin—will rebel against the atrocities of the Taiping, leading to an ironic situation: they are rebels from the point of view of both the imperial troops and the rulers of the Heavenly Kingdom.

Wang Lee and Mei Lin do not see themselves as rebels, however. In the final pages of the novel—the narrator having shifted to the first person plural—Wang Lee and Mei Lin assert their continuity with the principles of Feng and of the Heavenly Kingdom: "Today we endure only as a promise sealed in a wall."[11] The pronoun is telling, connecting them not only to each other but to others of similar mind in their movement. The novel ends then with a resolution of the ironic tensions of the title, focusing on the private will of two characters to be true to the hope and beliefs of their movement.

Much of the novel is a working out of the decay of the Taiping principles. When Wang Lee, Mei Lin, and Chu first come to the encampment, the scene is one of order, civility, mutual succor, plenty. They are greeted with offers of food and surrounded by happy families who are filled with a sense of purpose and community. But very quickly that Edenic image is tarnished by the activities of Yang, who, like a side-show charlatan, acts out a role to convince the gullible. From the moment Yang is able to convince the Taiping that God speaks through him, the movement has lost its purity and, with it, its purpose. From then on it becomes the drive to the consolidation of political power.

The first step is a small one. When the imperial forces attack the encampment, the Taiping drive them back. Astonished by the ease of their victory, they rejoice in their newfound strength. Even gentle Chu takes pride in the gun he has plundered. But what had been an army principally meant for defense becomes an offensive army, as Hung and Yang decide to establish their own dynasties. At first they respect the peasants and farmers; there is no destruction of crops. Nor are any of the defeated cities plundered. But inevitably, as the movement spirals downward, even these principles are lost, and cities are destroyed for no other reason than this is the will of God speaking through the kings. In its last stage the movement turns inward to feed on itself.

It would not have been difficult for Paterson to turn this into a novel of despair. Certainly on the large-scale public level the distinct suggestion is that movements, no matter how well motivated, do not remain pure. Principles are first established, then broadened, then rationalized into new understandings, and then simply abandoned. *Animal Farm* is played out in China.

But instead the novel is filled with tremendous hope—Paterson's great theme. It is not on the public level that principles are embraced; it is on the private level. It is individuals who bring about the Heavenly Kingdom, and what is quite moving about the novel's conclusion is that Wang Lee and Mei Lin are doing more to bring about the Heavenly Kingdom by literally cultivating their garden than they had as soldiers in the rebellion.

Paterson traces this most especially in Wang Lee, though Mei Lin and Chu will experience the same cycle of commitment and disillusionment that Wang Lee undergoes. The novel begins with Wang Lee being abducted by three somewhat silly but malicious bandits; he is not particularly upset. He will see the world. The depravities of the bandits and his separation from his parents do not shake his fundamental belief in the rightness of traditional ways.

When he is rescued by Mei Lin, his traditional prejudices blind him to new possibilities. He scorns Mei Lin for her unbound feet. He is humiliated by being rebuked by a woman. He disdains the learning that she offers. Despite all she represents, however, he grows to love her. This he must hide once the camp is divided by sex, and soon he is as firmly committed to the Taiping principles as he had been to his old traditions.

M. Sarah Smedman has pointed out that much of the novel focuses on the interplay between male and female roles. Mei Lin and Wang Lee are not infrequently disguised as members of the opposite sex, and Smedman sees Mei Lin coming to represent the masculine principle of spirit, Wang Lee coming to represent the feminine principle of soul. It is Wang Lee who is sick in his soul at the killing and who yearns with a great surging for the love of Mei Lin; it is Mei Lin who remains distant as the almost mythic embodiment of Taiping principles, the leopard colonel setting the standard. Smedman writes,

> The epilogue celebrates the union of spirit with soul. The celebration, however, is solemn, even sombre. Wang Lee and Mei Lin have learned with equanimity to live with ambiguity, to go on quietly, with the knowledge of their own, as well as society's, failure to live by the creeds they profess, even betrayal of those principles by transforming metaphorical truths into literalisms which then become untenable, blasphemous. . . . That bleak view is ameliorated by the knowledge that people like Mei Lin and Wang Lee will compensate for wrongheaded zealotry by doing what they can to make peace in their immediate environments.[12]

Smedman's suggestion adds power to the ending, where Wang Lee and Mei Lin are fruitful both in terms of childbearing and in terms of the land because of their union. That union does not discard the essential truths that they have lived by, but it does reject the fanaticism that makes those principles more important than persons.

To get to this point, Wang Lee must overcome his zealotry and look into his soul. For most of the novel he is committed unthinkingly. He never questions; he never probes. When his student Shen asks questions he cannot answer—questions that trouble his own unexamined life—Wang Lee first resorts to rote memory and then to silence. When Shen's studies lead him to conclude that Taiping principles demand that peace be established, Wang Lee responds with the greatest treachery of the novel: he denounces Shen, who is beheaded. The result is a kind of haunting: "Wang Lee took care not to see it, but it came to him in dreams, all the same. The eyes were wide open, staring at his face, and the lips were parted, as if in speech. The hair was brown and matted with blood, and sometimes there would be a single finger shaking slightly beside the nose. The boy would wake with a lurch and lean over to spit on the earth floor" (126). The head is not so much accusing; it is instead posed in the same way Shen had looked when he asked the troubling questions. They have not gone away;

in fact, they have become more acute. Wang Lee's response to the dream is telling: he reverts to his traditional superstitions.

Wang Lee closes his eyes to the blood, and the killing becomes easier and easier. At Chuan-chou the killing is not so easy, however. Having slaughtered through the night, he kills a mother protecting the entrance to her house. When he walks in, he sees a shadow move. He shoots and kills a two-year-old girl, "mother's milk still sweet upon her lips" (139). This is the major turning point. He walks to the river, strips, tries to wash away what he has become, tries to drown, and ends in despair and meaninglessness. The movement by which he had guided his life has led him to this. He is, the narrator suggests, "more weary than a graveless ghost" (140).

But this is not the end. In fact, Wang Lee begins to turn against both sets of traditions that have informed his life. He confesses his love to Mei Lin, who rejects him, for she is still committed to the principles of the Taiping. Later, when he is sent as a spy but sold as a slave in Changsha, Wang Lee sees the horror of the convention of binding feet; his prejudices melt away in the presence of a young girl whose feet are broken. His response suggests how far he has abandoned his traditions; he teaches her to read and write, something no woman, he once would have said, needed to know. When he escapes Changsa, he goes to find Mei Lin not as a soldier in the rebellion but as a lover. And this is how they find each other.

The ending of the book carries with it the promise of new life, the promise of hope. Wang Lee and Mei Lin return to his ancestral home, and they plant the seed rice hidden by his father behind the fifth brick in the northeast wall. The rice, a symbol of their new life and new hope, is replaced by a rosary, a symbol of the Heavenly Kingdom that the Taiping had promised but that for now remains a hope. It is a hope not without pain: the kingdom is gone, Wang Lee's parents have disappeared. But it is a real hope nonetheless, mirroring the hope that concludes *Of Nightingales That Weep*. In the last line of *Rebels of the Heavenly Kingdom* the hopes represented by the seed rice and the rosary are united: "Today we endure only as a promise sealed in a wall. Someday, perhaps, we shall take root in the earth" (227).

The suggestion of the novel is that hope is a very individual thing; at most it can be held by a family. It was not the Taiping's principles that caused the movement's decay but their enactment in the human world. Once they came down from the mountains, the Taiping were indistinguishable from their enemies. Once a king sets himself apart, he opens himself to the delusion of becoming a god. Once community is dissolved, there is the potential for the horror of a kingly son ordering the execution of his parents.

At the beginning of the novel Mei Lin tells Wang Lee her story—one of disgrace and degradation. But somehow, she muses, the Heavenly Kingdom had given her nobility, had given her hope. Chu, the narrator suggests, "never tired of hearing how those without hope had come into the Heavenly Kingdom" (45). *Rebels of the Heavenly Kingdom* is the story of those who, without hope, find it in places they had never anticipated, and thus begin their movement to the heavenly kingdom. It is, in short, an archetypal Katherine Paterson story.

3.

Prodigal Children in Search of Hope

In her historical fiction Katherine Paterson focuses on individuals taken away from their families—whether to a puppet theater, a royal court, the streets of a city, or to a mountain retreat. They react to this loss quite differently—sometimes with terrible shame, sometimes with terrible longing. Through the course of the novel each of the characters is in the process of looking for a home, looking for a family. It is such hope that often propels the action of the novel or, more accurately, that describes the course that the characters chart as the action swirls around them.

Bridge to Terabithia (1977) is often cited as Paterson's emergence into the genre of realism or—what is now seen as a misnamed genre—the problem novel. More notable is that with *Bridge to Terabithia* Paterson started to examine characters within the family structure. Often her characters strain at those family structures; the protagonists frequently feel outside the structures. But the impulses that guide the characters of her later realism are the same ones that guide her earlier characters—they want to find a home and to find themselves. For the characters of Katherine Paterson, these are not easy goals. Her characters are pilgrims along a narrow path; again and again she would use this archetypal journey in ways not dissimilar to those of John Bunyan. In addition though, these characters are prodigal children, desperate to find a home but beleaguered by their own fear. Most are like the frog that Triphena describes in *Lyddie:* they desperately kick at the milk they have fallen into in order to churn it into solid butter so that they will not drown.

Bridge to Terabithia

With *Bridge to Terabithia* Paterson turned to contemporary realism, and with that change came a new setting and a new sort of situation. The protagonists are younger than Paterson's previous heroes and heroines, and in some sense their situations are somewhat less desperate. Jessie Aarons faces some of the same difficulties faced by Muna and Jiro. He especially faces the need to accept himself. But whereas Muna searches for a family, Jessie must find a place for himself in a family where he does not appear to fit in. It is a complex and painful search.

Bridge to Terabithia won Paterson the 1978 Newbery Award. In her acceptance speech she focused on the notion of bridges, which are central to the book. In fact, she argued that the book might itself be a bridge "that will take children from where they are to where they might be" ("Newbury," 363). The bridge metaphor functions on several levels in this speech. The novel is a bridge over the chasm of death that Paterson felt. It is a way to overcome the chasms established by "time and culture and desperate human nature." It is a bridge to the promised land, allowing "the very valley where evil and despair defeat us . . . [to] become a gate of hope" ("Newbury," 367). This reference to hope and crossings would, of course, be familiar to readers of her earlier novels.

Bridge to Terabithia does focus on the notion of crossings. Jess Aarons is the most visible "crosser," though not the only one. In each case the crossing involves a movement from the most mundane, expected, humdrum way of the world into a realm of grace and high courtesy and imagination. It is a crossing made by Jess and Leslie. It is a crossing promised to May Belle and perhaps to Joyce Ann. And it is a crossing offered to those who at first seem to be the least likely crossers: Jess's father and his teacher, Mrs.

Myers. If these crossings define the growth of individual characters, they also define the growth of the family structures of those characters, especially as Jess's family comes to new awarenesses about their son's needs and their own willingness to show love.

The novel opens with a moment of hope for Jess: he will be the fastest runner in his school. His mother and older sisters do not find this to be even moderately interesting, though his two younger sisters do. As his father is away most of the time, Jess is responsible for many of the chores, which he does alone. In fact, he does almost everything alone.

At school, he is to be disappointed: Leslie Burke, a girl whose family has just moved into the house next door, is faster. In fact, she makes it clear that in many ways she does not know her place. She plays with the boys, she wears grubby clothes, she admits that she has no television, and she virtually insists on being his friend.

When Jess hears one of Leslie's papers read aloud, he recognizes in her the creativity and imagination that he feels but cannot express to his family. He also recognizes his growing friendship, as he tries to help her to do what he does: fit in without sticking out. Together, at first to escape from the world of their classroom, they create the kingdom of Terabithia, a land of high imagination. One can only enter by swinging across a dry creekbed.

As their friendship grows, Jess must face the questioning of his classmates and family. But Leslie has opened up the world of the imagination for him, and he is not the same insecure boy he once was. At Christmas he gives her a dog, Prince Terrian, and they rejoice in their imaginative world, in the sense that they can withdraw from the ugliness of the world around them, that they can understand life in a very different way. The bickering of Jess's older sisters, the disappointed cynicism of his father, and the stifling classroom can be put aside.

There is one teacher who can do for Jess something of what Leslie does: Miss Edmunds. When, on a rainy Saturday, she offers to take Jess to an art exhibit, he agrees gladly. When he returns, however, he finds his family waiting: Leslie has drowned in the swollen creek while trying to cross the gully into Terabithia. Stricken, Jess runs away. His father follows, and in a moment of unexpected grace and newfound love, he picks Jess up and carries him back to the pickup and their home. He cannot yet find the right words to connect with Jess, but he has found the right actions.

Jess is numb. His family cannot seem to understand his reaction, though they are gentle to him. He endures the funeral, the sympathies of his teacher, and the departure of Leslie's family. Even Prince Terrien will be gone. But Jess has grown, and he has taken on the imaginative capacities of Leslie. He, too, will become a bridge. He builds a crude crossing over the gully, and, when his younger sister May Belle comes to see, he brings her across into Terabithia—a land of milk and honey—and introduces her to a world ever so much more real: "And when he had finished, he put flowers in her hair and led her across the bridge—the great bridge into Terabithia—which might look to someone with no magic in him like a few planks across a nearly dry gully."[1]

It is a moment of consummate grace, a moment echoed in the conclusions of *Come Sing, Jimmy Jo, Park's Quest,* and *The Great Gilly Hopkins.* Jess has grown from a rather shy and somewhat lonely child with no close friends to a giver of grace. He is a boy placed in a stultifying school environment where the best strategy—a strategy Jimmy Jo uses—is to remain unobtrusive and unobserved. This is true with regard to both the teachers and other students. When at the opening of the novel Jess is convinced that he will be the fastest runner, he holds back from taking the lead in organizing the races and lets others sort things out. When he is caught drawing in class, his response is one of almost despair: "Jess's face was burning hot. He slid the notebook paper back under his desk top and put his head down. A whole year of this. Eight more years of this. He wasn't sure he could stand it" (23). In fact, there is almost no relief for Jess, except perhaps in the adoration of his younger sisters.

This is what makes his attack on Janice Avery so extraordinary. This retiring kid who is so anxious not to be noticed slights Janice in order to protect Leslie, thus calling himself to the attention of the school's bully. It is an instinctive response to protect his new friend. His growth has begun, but just begun. As he grows closer to Leslie, he grows in understanding of the demands of friendship. Eventually he and Leslie will be the ones who minister to a lonely Janice; they find her to be more needy, less self-assured and independent than they imagined. Their ministry—an act almost unthinkable at the beginning of the novel—is perhaps not totally unexpected; Jess's kindness to his somewhat ignored younger sister suggests this quality, but it takes Leslie to help him to respond in this way on the level of his peers.

At the conclusion of the novel Jess is no longer trying to set himself apart, either through averting his eyes from others' gazes or through establishing himself as his class's fastest runner. He is instead building bridges, making a way for others to participate in the imaginative world of Terabithia. This is the legacy of Leslie's friendship.

Leslie Burke is in one essential way precisely the opposite of Jess. Where he is inherently fearful and inward, burying his imaginative exploits, hiding his art, Leslie is outward-looking (though not extroverted), celebrating her imagination. She has an ambiguous relationship with these traits, at once a bit shy and discomforted by the way she appears to others and yet anxious to accentuate the distinctions. She is hurt by her classmates' disparaging rejection of her, yet she is completely aware of the differences responsible for her isolation. She innocently announces that her family has no television, she dresses quite differently (and by choice), and she almost naively shows herself to be the dominant runner, thus alienating herself from all the boys in the class. In fact, all of her classmates see her as intruding into spheres where she does not belong.

But Leslie is a girl with an imaginative vision; it is something Jess soon recognizes about her. She introduces the idea of Terabithia, and when she speaks, "the words rolling out so regally, you knew she was a proper queen" (40). When Jess tries to draw a picture of Terabithia, Leslie responds out of her own imaginative vision: "How could he explain it in a way Leslie would understand, how he yearned to reach out and capture the quivering life about him and how when he tried, it slipped past his fingertips, leaving a dry fossil upon the page? 'I just can't get the poetry of the trees,' he said" (40). His line suggests his own somewhat buried imaginative vision, and Leslie's response is telling: "Don't worry. . . . You will someday" (40). It is a moment of grace. It is perhaps the first real encouragement he has ever received. It is certainly the first encouragement he has ever received from a peer.

In fact, Leslie herself is the imaginative bridge into Terabithia. Jess fears the swing across the gully, but even more he fears the swing across into the place of imagination. It is not something his father would understand or approve of, nor would his teacher, Mrs. Myers. Leslie does more than establish an imaginary kingdom with Jess; she helps him to establish a whole way of looking at things: "For hadn't Leslie, even in Terabithia, tried to push back the walls of his mind and make him see beyond to the shining world—huge and terrible and beautiful and very fragile? . . . It was up to him to pay back to the world in beauty and caring what Leslie had loaned him in vision and strength" (126). And this is precisely what he does, as grace and the imaginative version merge, as he sets planks over a gully, and as he brings May Belle into a new land.

Jess and Leslie are not the only bridges in the novel. Certainly Miss Edmunds plays this role. She, like Leslie, is attuned to the artistic vision, and her music lifts Jess out of the strangling world. She tells him to keep drawing, and on one elementary level he draws for her. She is also the one who brings him to the Washington, D.C., art gallery, a place that strikes Jess as sacred: "He was drunk with color and form and hugeness" (100). She, like Leslie, pushes back the limits of possibilities.

There are also two unlikely bridges. Mrs. Myers, Jess comes to realize, is not just one element in a stultifying world. "Let's try to help each other, shall we?" (125), she asks Jess after Leslie's death. And in fact she does help him, for she recognizes that Jess will always remember Leslie. Perhaps she is the first—though not the only—adult who recognizes this.

The second unlikely bridge is Jess's father. Throughout the novel Jess is merely assumed by his father. Caught up in his own work, and then the lack thereof, he ignores Jess, provides no connection, never touches him; he forces Jess to hide what is most important to him. After Leslie's death, however, it is his father who comes after him in the truck and who picks him up—the first time he has touched him in the novel—"as though he were a baby" (104). Donna Diamond's illustration of this moment pictures them against Terabithian trees, and it is exactly right, for a connection has been made. It is an awkward connection: Jess's father does not know what to say. But it is a connection nonetheless.

It is his father who gently and with love brings Jess to the wake for Leslie's family. It is his father who gently keeps May Belle from intruding. It is his father who sits down with Jess after he has pitched Leslie's paints into the stream. "That was a damn fool thing to do," he says, but not with anger. He understands Jess's anger and grief. He pulls him onto his lap and soothes him, stroking his hair. "Hell, ain't it," he says to Jess, and Jess suddenly realizes the connection: "It was the kind of things Jess could hear his father saying to another man. He found it strangely comforting, and it made him bold" (116). A bridge has been built. And perhaps it is stronger than either of them realize at the time. After all, it is his paints and paper that Jess's father says should not have been thrown away. It is as though he is willing to affirm Jess's gifts.

This is an enormous change; in a sense, Jess has been a bridge for his father as well, a father who had earlier denigrated Jess's desire to draw. Now, however, there are connections between them. It had been a scattered family, with few connections. Jess's two older sisters whine their way into laziness; Jess's mother and father are too worn out to show much concern. May Belle and Joyce Ann are too young to be real companions for Jess. Jess himself is the only one who tries to make connections between some of these isolated units; in the end, some bridges are indeed built, though gullies remain.

Leslie's family, in contrast, seems much closer. They are not under the same financial pressures as Jess's, and, at least partially because of that, they are not ground down by constant worry. They explore things that would never occur to Jess's family to explore—music and art. For Jess's family, these things are extrane-

From Katherine Paterson, *Bridge to Terabithia.* Illustration by Donna Diamond. Copyright © 1977 by Katherine Paterson. Used by permission of HarperCollins Publishers.

ous and impractical. For Leslie's, they are some of the dearest parts of life. Jess responds somewhat sheepishly to this; he cannot bring himself to see these interests as quite normal.

What brings these families together for the first and only time is one of the most elemental parts of life: death. This is a mutual grief that is almost startling. Jess's father's constant reference to the "little girl" that God would never doom to hell suggests how he sees Jess—as a young child. Jess's family has feared that he too, had drowned, and he is given back to them as a gift beyond price—as, indeed, all children are.

Jess has grown in the novel: we start in a muddy field among lazy cows and end in Terabithia. Jess has had his imaginative vision affirmed. He has been introduced to whole new worlds of imaginative possibilities. He has seen the union of the imagination with grace. He started out wanting to be the fastest runner in the fifth grade (a goal he achieves); he ends up something so much more.

There is a strong suggestion in *Bridge to Terabithia*—stronger than in Paterson's earlier historical fiction—that there are stories yet untold here. There are Leslie's parents who reject social expectations. There is Jess's father who has buried sensitivity and love until death digs it up. There is May Belle who yearns for love. There is Janice Avery who bullies others to hide her pain. And Mrs. Myers who cries at the loss of her student. Readers see the story from a single, limited perspective; other perspectives, though they will impinge on the story's primary perspective, remain largely hidden and unknowable. This is what Jess learns when he befriends Janice Avery. Perhaps part of Jess's growth is his ability to see those other perspectives and to build bridges based on those new understandings.

The Great Gilly Hopkins

Though *Bridge to Terabithia* deals with the structure of the family, it does so in the context of an established family. In *The Great Gilly Hopkins* (1978) Paterson examines a broken family set against a family in the making. At the center of this novel is a prodigal child looking for a family—a consideration that dominates a number of Paterson's later novels, most notably *Come Sing, Jimmy Jo* and *Park's Quest*. Like the Prodigal Son, Gilly is, after so many mistakes, desperately searching for a family. And then, against all hope, she finds one—the one she had least expected. Gilly is the prodigal come home, though perhaps not to the home she had imagined. Nevertheless, it is a home that had been there for her (and for her mother, Courtney, who is another prodigal child in this story) all along, though she has never known of it.

The novel opens with Gilly being driven by her social worker to her new foster home. Having been abandoned several times in the past, she is not hopeful and has steeled herself into a kind of brutal antagonism. She is unprepared for the great earth mother that is Maimie Trotter. She is introduced into a strange household: Maimie, her foster son, William Ernest, and Mr. Randolph, a blind neighbor. Gilly is aghast at all of them: the fat mother, the weird and frightened kid, and a black neighbor, whose hand she will not take.

She resolves to control them all, but her devices fail. Trotter will not call her on her disheveled hair, will not rise to arguments, and will not give in or be controlled. Gilly is similarly unsuccessful at school, where her new teacher, Miss Harris, recognizes her considerable gifts but also recognizes her even more considerable anger. Gilly can only control Agnes Stokes, a toadie whose control gives no pleasure. Resolving to flee, Gilly writes a letter filled with fabricated desperation to her mother, the beautiful Courtney, who, she firmly believes, loves her and wants to be with her.

But the thing that Gilly had least expected to happen, happens. She is loved. When, partly out of deception but also partly out of a growing love, she is kind to William Ernest, she fears that her strength, born out of the anger of abandonment, will be sapped away:

> For a moment Gilly looked at [Trotter], then quickly turned away as a person turns from bright sunlight. . . . [Gilly] took [Mr. Randolph's] elbow and guided him carefully down the stairs, taking care not to look back over her shoulder because

> the look on Trotter's face was the one Gilly had, in some deeper part of her, longed to see all her life, but not from someone like Trotter. That was not part of the plan.[2]

Fearing that the plan will come unraveled, she arms herself against love, and, using William Ernest, she steals money from Mr. Randolph and runs to the bus station.

But she is stopped. Maimie brings her back home, defends her against the social worker, and incorporates her back in to the family. She returns principally because William Ernest has grown to love her. And most astonishingly, she has grown to love him. They become a family, and Gilly becomes just as nurturing to William Ernest as Trotter.

But the letter Gilly has written bears its fruit. Courtney does not come, but she sends her mother, who takes Gilly away. The pain for all of them is almost unbearable, but Trotter enjoins her to make her proud. And Gilly quickly sees that Nonnie, her grandmother, is the parent who always watched for but never saw the prodigal child return home. They, too, grow close. But when Courtney announces that she is coming, Gilly is overwhelmed. The beautiful Courtney is coming.

But it is a coming filled with enormous disappointment. Courtney is, in Gilly's words, "a flower child gone to seed" (145). She has come for only two days. She has come only because Nonnie has sent her money. Paterson has suggested that if she were to tell Courtney's story, we would love her and ache for her (Interview). But this is hard to imagine. Gilly is devastated and calls Trotter to announce that she is coming—and this is a significant word—"home." But Trotter shows her that she is home, and that life is neither fair nor easy. Trotter says, "Sometimes in this world things come easy, and you tend to lean back and say, 'Well, finally, happy ending. This is the way things is supposed to be.' Like life owed you good things. . . . And there is lots of good things, baby. . . . But you just fool yourself if you expect good things all the time. They ain't what regular—don't nobody owe 'em to you" (148). Gilly returns to her grandmother and mother, determined to make Trotter proud.

The lines Gilly thinks of as she returns to Courtney are Wordsworth's, those she had read earlier with Mr. Randolph[3]:

> Not in entire forgetfulness,
> And not in utter nakedness, . . .
> But trailing clouds of glory do we come
> From God, who is our home. . . .

It does not seem at the beginning of the novel that Gilly is arriving at a new home, trailing clouds of glory. In fact, she trails clouds of pain. Having been abandoned by her mother, she has also been abandoned by one family who had promised to keep her but had then left her out with the trash when they left for Florida, and by another family who had simply been unable to handle her. Gilly's response is to manipulate others by drawing on the anger of abandonment. As Miss Harris, one of her teachers, suggests, Gilly's "anger is still up here on the surface where you can look it in the face, make friends with it if you want to" (59). She does indeed; it is her source of strength.

What Gilly cannot face is her anger at her mother. Having fabricated a fantasy about her, she distributes her anger elsewhere. But whereas before she had made people treat her as a special case, she is unable to do this with either Miss Harris or Trotter. Neither Miss Harris nor Trotter depend on others for how they see themselves; they will not let Gilly define them or fix them in specific roles. What Gilly first identifies as her own oncoming softness is in fact their strength.

Miss Harris is the cool and competent professional. She recognizes Gilly's intellectual gifts but also the anger that drives those gifts. As an African-American she also identifies with the anger. She has a real concern for Gilly, as a later letter she sends suggests. She recognizes what Anne Shirley of *Anne of Green Gables* would call a kindred spirit. The reader never discovers if Gilly comes to recognize that kinship.

Trotter is anything but cool, though she is more than competent. Her large size, her absolutely unbounded capacity for love, her sense of protectiveness, her refusal to accept being merely a "foster" mother—all suggest her status as a kind of earth mother. Paterson has suggested that she drew both Maime Trotter and Gilly larger than life deliberately to make her point.[4] This is certainly true of Trotter. When Gilly first arrives and Trotter tells the social worker that she has never found a child she was unable to be friends with, she is actually diminishing what she truly does. She loves them, totally and without reserve. She does not show this through good housekeeping or through physical beauty; she shows it at first in the only way Gilly allows her to show it: through food. Each meal is a family festival, filled with intense affirmation.

Gilly recognizes early on that the way to Trotter's heart is through William Ernest, and in part this is true. Gilly has been toughened by loss, and she has used her anger to grow strong. But William Ernest has also experienced loss and pain, and he has not been toughened. He has become fearful and withdrawn; he hides behind Trotter's more than ample protection. Trotter gives all the protection her love can give. Though she quite senses the necessity of William Ernest becoming tougher, she can hardly endure it. Life is tough work, she later tells Gilly, and one can take pride in doing a good job at it.[5] But behind that sentiment lies an infinite sadness that the world is as it is, that little children need to be toughened against life's slings and arrows.

William Ernest is at first dreadfully afraid of Gilly. He does not recognize the deception she plays on him when she pretends to help him. But neither does she recognize that the deception becomes reality, as by grace it sometimes does. As she helps him with his reading, watches "Sesame Street" with him, and crafts a paper airplane for him—her best ever—she grows to love him. Eventually she will take on the role of his protector at school. She will be the one to give him boxing lessons to toughen him and to care for him when he is ill over Thanksgiving. Having begun by using him, she ends by ministering to him, and loving him, and being loved in return. This is why Gilly responds to his plea to come home. He asks her to come because he loves her. If Gilly is not yet able to accept sincerity from an adult, she is able to accept it from a child. And though in this scene she may hide, both from herself and others, her own desperate need to be loved, the reader senses it.

This is the beginning of the formation of a family—a family in which all love and need to be loved.

Mr. Randolph is part of that family as well. Virtually blind, he eats his dinners at Trotter's home. He is the kind of person whom Gilly could easily despise. He is dependent; he seems to lack her strength. But in fact he is just the opposite. He refuses to lose his independence to his son or to allow his handicap to lead to any kind of despair. Perhaps most significant is his ability to accept love—offered, once again, by Trotter. This is something Gilly does not understand: that an acceptance of love is not weakness. It is part of the web of charity that holds the family together, and Gilly herself will come to be able to offer this kind of love.

Mr. Randolph also represents a love of art that has escaped Gilly. In the past she has used her skills in reading as a kind of weapon, manipulating her teachers and showing herself superior to her peers. But she is strangely moved by Mr. Randolph's ability to recall Wordsworth: "The music of the words rolled up and burst across Gilly like waves upon a beach" (38). After the reading she refuses to acknowledge the power of Wordsworth's poem, but she remembers the poem right up to the end of the novel, so that the "clouds of glory" come to be important for her own understanding of herself and her situation. When she returns to Courtney at the airport, she muses that there are "no clouds of glory, perhaps, but Trotter would be proud" (148). (She does not see the clouds, but they are there.) It is not surprising that Mr. Randolph, who also is a giver of love, gives the anthology of poems that Gilly had read from to her as a parting gift.

The principal motif of the novel is that of the returning prodigal child. But it is not a retelling that ends with feasts and fatted calves. It is a story where pain and loss mingle with joy and hope—the same kind of ending that concludes *Bridge to Terabithea, Come Sing, Jimmy Jo, Park's Quest,* and *Lyddie.* The reluctant presence of Courtney at the airport reminds the reader that not all prodigals do return home; the broken relationship is not healed. (It is a relationship so broken that Gilly, who knows nothing of the tensions between Courtney and Nonnie, cannot make herself stay in Courtney's old room; she chooses the room of an uncle killed in Vietnam.) But Gilly has returned home.

It is a home that Gilly and Nonnie must forge, and the novel concludes on a note of tremendous hope. Gilly will remain with Nonnie not because of Courtney, but because of the new web of charity established between Nonnie and Gilly. Having learned the lessons of structuring a family, of accepting and giving love, she is able to work toward the construction of that web. She is even able, at the novel's close, to articulate her love for Trotter.

Gilly learns these lessons under the tutelage of someone she had at first despised but who is in fact skilled in the ways of love. Claudia Mills has pointed out the stark distinction between the first meeting of Trotter and Gilly and that of Anne Shirley and Marilla in *Anne of Green Gables.* In L. M. Montgomery's text, Anne chatters away to the quiet Matthew about coming to a real, beautiful home, about coming to Green Gables for a family, though the reader knows all along that from Marilla's point of view this has been a big mistake. But from the first moment Trotter sees Gilly, she accepts her, and it is the "orphan" who sees the encounter as a horrible mistake.[6] Later, when Gilly realizes that she must leave Trotter, she is devastated. But Trotter comes to her, and holds her, and rubs her enormous hand up and down Gilly's back. She is truly at this point Gilly's mother, holding her as she holds William Ernest. Despite the pain of her loss, Trotter is still able to give love. It is a lesson not lost on Gilly, who will repeat it later, at the airport.

In Paterson's work a reader sees only a portion of a much larger story. Gilly senses that she knows very little about her larger story; she had not even imagined that she had a grandmother, or that her own mother would grow older. Paterson structures the novel to suggest that sense of limitation. She pulls the narrator back, allowing the reader only Gilly's limited perspective, and then presents a series of scenes, not always connected by transitions, that show in stark visual images Gilly's hostility slowly transformed to love. She begins with Gilly's bubble-gummed hair and then paints pictures of the first meeting, the family at dinner, the reading of Wordsworth, holding Mr. Randolph's hand instead of his elbow, Trotter rubbing Gilly's back, the ride in Nonnie's car. Perhaps the most visually striking scene comes during Nonnie's visit, when Mr. Randolph is lying sick in the living room, William Ernest comes down having wet his pajamas, and Trotter, faint from illness, falls atop a distraught Gilly, who, lovingly and frenetically, watches over them all. It is on the one hand a vaudevillian scene, a comedy of errors. On the other hand it is a powerful visual image of how far Gilly has come in her ability to love and administer love.

Each scene suggests visually what is not readily apparent in the text: Gilly's growth. The reader sees it even before Gilly does. The limited narrative stance, which Paterson would limit even more strictly in *Jacob Have I Loved,* enhances the power of the visual images, creating meaning for the reader that is not there for the characters. At the end, Gilly's realization of her growth comes as something of a shock to her—but not to the reader.

Gilly's growth Paterson suggests by the girl's name. Galadriel, as Gilly learns for the first time from Miss Harris, is the beautiful elven queen who holds one of the rings of power in Tolkien's *Lord of the Rings* trilogy. Gilly does not allow Miss Harris to call her Galadriel; to do so would be to yield some slight advantage, and Gilly will not choose to yield anything. Yet although Gilly had not known the reference, she yearns to be the beautiful lady living with the beautiful Courtney. To her mind, Courtney is Galadriel. But she discovers that love will not come from the beautiful Courtney but instead from the un-beautiful Trotter in a dusty house with little money. Frodo could not stay with Galadriel; neither can Gilly. She defines herself quite differently.

Gilly's last name comes from the poet Gerard Manley Hopkins, whom Paterson will periodically quote in her essays. Perhaps there is no more significance to this choice than the pleasure of the author. But when one thinks of the poet's description of himself in "The Windhover" as having a "heart in hiding" that becomes deeply stirred, or when one thinks of the image in "God's Grandeur" of the Holy Ghost brooding over the bent world, it is hard not to think of Gilly and Trotter in a bent world filled with loss and abandonment, where prodigals may fall away but where they may also, against all hope, find themselves in a family.

Angels and Other Strangers

The year after *The Great Gilly Hopkins* was published, Paterson saw the publication of *Angels and Other Strangers* (1979), a collection of nine Christmas stories that had originally been prepared for a church setting. These stories are reminiscent of Flannery O'Connor's, for in each a character is caught in a moment where the world seemingly—and sometimes not so seemingly—is malevolent and threatening, where characters could easily give in to despair. And yet, suddenly, like the flash of the Christmas star, grace enters their lives, and the world that had been so desperate is full of peace and hope.

It is, of course, an old formula to set a story full of hope during Christmastide. Films like *A Miracle on Thirty-fourth Street, It's a Wonderful Life, Holiday Inn,* and the many screen versions of Charles Dickens' *Christmas Carol* remind us of the convention every holiday season. Any story placed within this context is threatened by sentimentality. What saves Paterson's stories from this charge is their gritty, sometimes dark realism. Like Flannery O'Connor's stories, the moments of grace and revelation here are preceded by a descent into hell. She frequently concludes with a character beginning the ascent.

In "Angels and Other Strangers" Julia Thompson, forced to pick up a quarrelsome and irritating aunt on a snowy Christmas Eve, is helped by Jacob when she runs out of gas. Although he is walking 30 miles to spend his Christmas with a granddaughter, he will not ask for her help, sensing her fearfulness and distrust. But Julia comes to recognize him for what he is: a Christmas angel, and she offers grace for grace. In "Guests" Pastor Nagai offers a Christmas service in Japan during the war, despite the danger of worshiping the "American God." When a young girl comes, all alone, he tells her the story, even continuing when a policeman comes to take notes. In "Many Happy Reruns" Elizabeth comes to recognize God's love through the ministries of old Miss Violet, as do the children of "Maggie's Gift," who come to Mr. McGee's poor home to spend a Christmas away from the children's home. In "Woodrow Kennington Works Practically a Miracle," both Woodrow and his sister Sara Jane come to recognize God's acceptance and love as represented in the Nativity.

Many of the stories focus on adult reconciliations. In "Tidings of Joy" Carol begins to accept the loss of her baby when she comes to understand that Jesus' birth represented God's loss. "Star of Night" depicts another retelling of the prodigal son, merged with the story of the Magi. Here Carl comes to find his son and finds himself in a dilapidated house, fighting for the life of his grandson. "He Came Down" follows Lydia's growth in understanding how Jesus came to the poor and lowly, as "Broken Windows" follows a similar growth in the life of the minister of a wealthy congregation.

The Christmas seasons works as a catalyst in each of these tales. Suddenly the characters are forced to reevaluate conceptions that they had held unquestioningly for years. Julia Thompson learns to accept grace from a black stranger. Carol comes past her anger at God for her loss. Lydia sees that God's love is not wasted on the poor. Pastor Nagai rejects the fear that had paralyzed him for so long. In each case it is a new understanding of the meaning of Christmas that initiates the reevaluation.

When the soldier comes, presumably to arrest Pastor Nagai, the minister is overwhelmed by the wonder of the Christmas story. He invites his persecutor in: "'If you'll just sit there in the front with the child. . . .' He looked straight into the proud face. To Pastor Nagai's surprise he found it to be a young face. The eyes above the sneering mouth shifted slightly under the pastor's gaze. It is only a child, the pastor realized, another child who has never heard the story."[7] He opens his text and then recites the Christmas story from memory, concluding with the angels' command to the shepherds, "Fear not." "For the first time in many years," the story concludes, "Pastor Nagai obeyed the angel's word" (25). He has come to a new understanding of the power of the story, and he has come to see that story is so important that telling it invalidates his fears.

Many of the stories conclude when a character suddenly sees a line—often a familiar line from one of the carols—in a completely new guise. Lydia recognizes the significance of the familiar line from "Once in Royal David's City": "He came down to earth from heaven." Philip, the minister in "Broken Windows," comes to learn the meaning of the creedal phrase, "He descended into Hell": "And just for a while, maybe for just this once in Philip's usually proper and comfortable life, God had let him be there too" (118). "Didn't you let me catch a glimpse of your glory?" (118), he asks God, and the linking of hell with glory suggests Philip's new awarenesses.

Some stories climax in a subtle linguistic change that suggests enormous meanings. Carol moves from the oppression of an accusing dream— "Serves you right!"—to an understanding that in a world of suffering and death from which no one is immune, she must learn to care for others, "to serve them right." Mr. McGee, dealing with a young Gilly Hopkins, recognizes that, as Genevieve says, Jesus "was a foster kid before he was even born" (63).

The descent into hell that Philip endures is a process most of the characters in these stories must also endure. In fact, it is a process that Gilly would recognize, as would Jess, Wang Lee, and Muna. It is a process that inspires growth. The characters of *Angels and Other Strangers* begin their ascent away from hell through acts of service. These may be as minor as giving someone a ride to Washington, D.C., or as dramatic as killing a rat to protect a child. The acts of service come about when characters overcome an inner focus that blurs out the rest of the world. For Carol this means dropping her baseless guilt and anger, for Julia it means dropping her fear of Jacob, for Pastor Nagai it means dropping his fear of reprisal so that he might tell the story to yet another child.

In short, these are all prodigals who escape not from pigpens but from comfort to return home. They all must realize with the writer of "Once in Royal David's City" that "with the poor, the meek, and lowly / Lived on earth our Savior holy." Or they must learn with Louise of *Jacob Have I Loved* that God attends to, as the writer of "I Wonder as I Wander" suggests, the "poor on'ry people." And by grace, this is what Paterson's characters discover.

Jacob Have I Loved

Paterson won her second Newbery Award with *Jacob Have I Loved* (1980), a novel whose central characters are quite distinct from those of the first Newbery winner, *Bridge to Terabithea.* Growing up on the island of Rass, in the Chesapeake Bay, Louise is not so far geographically from Jess Aarons. But spiritually she is a world apart. Consumed with jealousy, Louise seems to condemn herself to a smaller and smaller world—one that shrinks almost as fast as the island of Rass. Whereas Jess's world expands, Louise's contracts. Whereas Jess reaches out, Louise closes down.

But they do have one thing in common, the same thing that all of Katherine Paterson's characters have: a need for a place or, at the very least, hope that a place can be found. Like Gilly and Jess, Louise is a prodigal, wandering willfully away in search of the home she has left. Not until the end of the novel does she recognize that what she has really been searching for has been right there all along. An all-consuming jealousy has generated a pain so intense as to distort everything that lies around her.

The novel begins in the present, as Louise comes to Rass Island, perhaps for the final time, to collect her mother and bring her to live with her family in the mountains. But the scene quickly shifts to 1941, when Louise is growing up on the Chesapeake Bay with her twin sister, Caroline. She is learning the ways of the watermen, and unlike most of the women on the island, she sees herself as following the water. But her sister shows no interest in the water. Beautiful and talented, she is someone that Louise envies to the point that she cherishes those few moments when she had been born before Caroline, though they are moments no one seems to remember.

But everyone remembers Caroline. Everyone seems to be willing to sacrifice for her—even Louise. The resentment that builds in Louise is enormous, and she vents it by interpreting all of Caroline's actions as slights. She cannot accept Caroline's light-hearted comments as anything but slurs; she hardly can visualize Caroline's moments of grace and giving as anything but self-centered. She can see nothing beyond the confines of her own limited and limiting perspective.

Still, Louise can recognize Caroline's talent, especially during one Christmas concert when she sings a lonely carol:

> I wonder as I wander out under the sky
> Why Jesus the Savior did come for to die
> For poor on'ry people like you and like I
> I wonder as I wander—out under the sky.[8]

Louise is almost shattered by the sound, but she is, until the end of the novel, unable to make any connections between its meaning and her own life. She will continue to see Caroline as set apart, and herself as one of the "poor on'ry people," not recognizing that the carol suggests that it is just these people for whom Jesus the Savior came for to die. So her resentment will grow.

When Hiram Wallace returns mysteriously to Rass after a 50-year absence, he causes a noticeable stir. Louise is at first convinced that he is a spy, and she enlists the aid of her friend Call to find him out. What they find instead is a lonely and loving man who wants to make a home for himself. Call and Louise help him rebuild the old Wallace home, though as Call grows closer and closer to "the Captain," Louise fears that she will lose her only friend. Her joy in the relationship is killed, so that when Call and the Captain go to clear Trudy Braxton's house of cats, she follows only with anger and resentment.

During a storm the Captain's house is washed completely away. Rowing with the Captain over the flooded site, Louise is overcome with sorrow and, then, with her growing sexuality. She reaches for him and clasps him tightly. But she is mortified by what she has done as she imagines what the Captain might think—and what others might think. When the Captain moves in with them, having no house, Louise can hardly meet his eyes. Only Louise's aging and cranky grandmother guesses, and, in her intemperance, she hatefully accuses Louise. No one accords her charges any seriousness, but Louise knows they are true.

Caroline comes up with the notion that the Captain might marry Trudy Braxton so that they might live together in her house. Louise is appalled, principally because Caroline seems to be moving in on her relationship with the Captain. But the Captain agrees, and so does Trudy. After the wedding Call and Caroline visit them frequently, but Louise cannot. She imagines that they have shut her out, but quite the opposite is true.

Call leaves school to work on the water with Louise's father, and almost at the same time the Captain is able to use a legacy left by Trudy (she dies soon after the marriage) to send Caroline to a good school for voice lessons. Louise is filled with resentment. When her parents offer to send her to a school as well, she does not see the grace with which the offer is made. She interprets it as them trying to be rid of her. So Caroline leaves, and Call leaves for the army, and Louise is alone.

Though not quite alone. She takes Call's place on her father's boat, and there she begins to find some peace, though perhaps not a place. As the months go by she resolves that she will follow the water, although she is a woman. She will stay in Rass and grow old and odd. But when Call returns, she is attracted to him for perhaps the first time, and she imagines that life need not be so lonely. Yet it is too late. Call has asked Caroline to marry him, and once again Louise is alone.

It is the Captain who finally brings things to a head, when he makes Louise shift her perspective. He makes her move away from a comparison of herself with Caroline to a focus on what she wants herself. Mountains, she decides, and to be a doctor. But she is afraid to leave. She is afraid to climb out from her sister's shadow—the identity she has made for herself. It is her mother who gives the release. We will miss you, her mother tells her, even more than we have missed Caroline. And now she can leave.

She goes to college, determined to be a doctor. But when her advisor tells her she will not be admitted to medical school, she moves to the University of Kentucky to become a nurse/midwife.

From there she moves to the small town of Truitt, surrounded by mountains. And there she finds her place.

The novel ends with a replay of Louise's own birth. She helps to bring a pair of twins into the world. The first comes easily, as she had, but the second is a difficult birth, and afterwards Louise struggles to keep the baby alive, just as her mother and grandmother had struggled to keep Caroline alive. Then Louise, after bringing that second child safely through, realizes that, like her, the first had been set aside. It was in no danger, so needed no attention. Louise tells the mother to hold and nurse the firstborn, and then picks up the second (Caroline's match) and nurses it at her own breast, filled with milk for her own newborn son. And then, late that night, walking home through the snow, she hears again the carol that her sister had sung so long ago.

The story of Caroline and Louise is modeled on that of Jacob and Esau, and though there is no moving reconciliation scene as there is in the biblical tale, there is a strong sense that Louise must deal with many of the tensions that Esau must have faced. Like Esau, Louise is the elder, but she does not seem, from her perspective, to be the more favored. (That this is not the case is irrelevant to her, given the unyielding perspective from which she looks.) It is Jacob who seems to follow the ways of the Lord, no matter that he is something of a scoundrel. It is Esau who seems cheated out of his birthright, no matter that he gave it away. It is Jacob that God loves and Esau that God hates. The love and the hate both seem utterly arbitrary, and Louise resigns herself, as Esau, she imagines, must have, to God's hate, unmerited and whimsical though it might be.

In her exploration of Paterson's use of literary allusion, M. Sarah Smedman argues that "literary allusion allows Paterson to communicate revealed truths which she perceives as offering hope and joy in realistic fictions which explore the meanings and *modus operandi* of those truths in concrete worlds of suffering, fear, and helplessness" (Smedman 1989, 59). Smedman goes on to suggest that such allusion contributes to the transformation of tragedy into romance and comedy.[9] This argument is particularly telling in *Jacob Have I Loved,* which uses the mythic story of

Jacob and Esau to examine the destructive relationship that Louise builds and to overturn the literal meaning of the myth in favor of a stronger truth about "poor on'ry people like you and like I." If she is Esau, she is also Jacob. But this knowledge will come only with maturity, and it will almost shatter her with its meaning and force.

For a long time Louise is unable to escape the destructive context in which she has placed herself. Imagining herself as Esau, she can only look with impotent jealousy on the favor shown her sister. Nothing seems to shake this perspective, and she will reinterpret events to affirm, but never to question, that perspective. When Caroline sings the carol, Louise is disgusted by what she perceives as Caroline's smugness, forgetting that she herself had almost been shattered by the beauty of the song. When Caroline rescues the 16 cats that Louise had wanted to save, she cannot be glad but only jealous of Caroline's winning ways. When the Captain tries to understand her—"'Sara Louise,' he was saying gently. 'What's wrong, my dear?'" (167)—she can only rush out of the "terrible house" (167), a house full of light and love. She rejects the grace given to "poor on'ry people."

Only when she works on the boat with her father is the destructive power of this Esau context alleviated somewhat.

> I was not happy in any way that would make sense to most people, but I was, for the first time in my life, deeply content with what life was giving me. Part of it was the discoveries—who would have believed that my father sang while tonging? . . . And he would serenade the oysters of Chesapeake Bay with the hymns the brothers Wesley had written to bring sinners to repentance and praise. Part of my deep contentment was due, I'm sure, to being with my father, but part, too, was that I was no longer fighting. My sister was gone, my grandmother a fleeting Sunday apparition, and God, if not dead, far removed from my concern. (187–88)

The sense of aloneness, of being the rejected and unfavored one, is alleviated by her father's companionship—a quiet, unassuming companionship. Here she learns things about her father she had never known, things that will have such an impact on her as to affect her choice of a husband. But her sense of rejection is not really over; there has been no reconciliation. She has stopped consciously fighting, and the sense of rejection has been buried, but it has been buried only by negation. Those she has been fighting against are no longer there to fight. And the work is tiring. She can hardly think about the others.

But in fact they are still there, waiting to be reconciled. Or perhaps it might be better to say that Louise has still not recognized that if she is to fulfill her own desperate need of grace, she must learn to accept grace when it is offered. This is no easy task for Esau, who does not see himself as one who may receive grace.

Jacob Have I Loved is Paterson's first use of the first-person narrative voice—a voice she had earlier rejected as being too self-absorbed. But it is, of course, precisely the right narrative perspective to use in a novel about a character who can see only one perspective. As such, it is also Paterson's first use of an unreliable narrator. The other characters seem unable to understand Louise's sense of isolation. Caroline asks if she is going crazy, the Captain tries to break through the walls Louise has established, her parents try to show their love, but Louise, the self-absorbed narrator, tells the events in a way that forces the reader to reevaluate the events Louise chronicles and see her own distortions.

Louise uses the distortion to narrow her world, to close off the favored ones—the ones she is not, the ones that hate her. She forces herself to be Esau, not knowing that, especially to her parents, she might actually be Jacob. Her life seems to be like that of Rass, getting smaller and smaller until, like Trudy or her grandmother, Louise will be boxed into a small house, fearful of the raging waves. Rass has a tightly knit island community, but as an island it is isolating and isolated. It is destructive and destroying, as storms take Louise's favorite driftwood stump and announce that the watermen's way of life on Rass is doomed. Caroline Goforth sees in the island a perverted home, where characters look inward to stunted growth. Truitt represents a real home—still an island, but a real home that looks outward, that invites others in.[10] The conclusion of the novel's prelude—"I love Rass Island, although for much of my life, I did not think I did" (4)—spoken in the present, suggests Louise's reconciliation with her past, her sister, and herself—a reconciliation that has led to Louise's mature self in another islandlike home.

The most powerful image of Louise's closing down is the oyster: "A live oyster, a good one, when it hits the culling board has a tightly closed shell. You throw away the open ones. They're dead already. I was a good oyster in those days. Not even the presence at Christmastime of a radiant, grown-up Caroline could get under my shell" (189–90). Her self-consciousness about the shell suggests, at the very least, that she is aware of the narrowing of her world, as she is aware that the island is itself getting smaller. Her reference to herself as a good oyster may be read as self-deprecating, given her distance from all of this (she tells the story as a memory), but it also sounds self-satisfied.

The result of this narrowing is that she withdraws from relationships, and not only the relationship with her sister. She withdraws from the Captain when Call becomes friendly with him. She withdraws from Trudy Braxton after her marriage to the Captain. There is no hint that she goes to see Caroline and Call after their marriage. In anger she claims that she hates everyone at school and that they hate her, though, as she admits to herself, this is not strictly true. She practices a withdrawal into isolation. She is a good oyster.

She is such a good oyster, in fact, that it is difficult for her to imagine closeness. She is angry at Caroline for suggesting that the Captain and Trudy should marry, but the real difficulty comes when she finds that a genuine tenderness exists between the two. She is unable to imagine that Call and Caroline might fall in love, and instead of rejoicing when it happens she interprets it as an act of malice against her. She is even jealous of the closeness between her parents, especially after they return from Caroline's wedding, their first trip together off the island:

> They seemed glad enough to see me, but I could tell that they weren't quite ready to let go of their time together. I carried

> one of the suitcases and lagged behind them in the narrow street. Occasionally, one or the other of them would turn and smile at me to say something like "Everything go all right?" but they walked closer together than they needed to, touching each other as they walked every few steps and then smiling into each other's faces. My teeth rattled, I was shivering so. (220)

Unable to accept love, unable to give it, she is also unable to endure seeing it in others. She shivers at the married couples around her. She is not such a good oyster after all.

Louise resolves to become a Trudy Braxton, but she is more quickly turning into her grandmother, a woman disappointed in love and insanely angry at the life she seems to have been allotted. It is not hard to imagine Louise repeating her pattern. And perhaps she will not be saved by the miracle—the Captain—that comes into Trudy's life.

It is her mother's simple declaration of love that enables Louise to break this cycle. Aware that she is loved, she can leave the shrinking that was the only thing she could cling to in the apparent absence of love. And when she leaves, she leaves to find her place. And when her father dies, her mother comes to live with Louise, not Caroline. Esau has rejected a terrible birthright, and another prodigal child has found a home.

With her mother's declaration, she is free to make a choice, to choose hope. One is reminded her of the final lines of John Steinbeck's *East of Eden,* where Cal is finally given a chance to choose his life, not to have it thrust on him. In choosing to leave Rass, Louise affirms that life is not dictated for her, that she may make a life apart from all that has gone before, that she may "begin to build myself as a soul" (228). This is what the Captain has done in choosing to return to Rass. And it is what Louise's mother has done. "'I chose the island,' she said. 'I chose to leave my own people and build a life for myself somewhere else. I certainly won't deny you that same choice'" (227). It is perhaps the first time Louise realizes she has a choice. It is at the least the first time she realizes that choosing a life does not mean rejection, but affirmation.

In fact, Louise must go beyond the bound life she sees evidenced in the crabs she catches:

> Shedding its shell is a long and painful business for a big Jimmy, but for a she-crab, turning into a sook, it seemed somehow worse. I'd watch them there in the float, knowing once they shed that last time and turned into grown-up lady crabs there was nothing left for them. They hadn't even had a Jimmy make love to them. Poor sooks. They'd never take a trip down the Bay to lay their eggs before they died. The fact that there wasn't much future for the Jimmies once they were packed in eelgrass didn't bother me so much. Males, I thought, always have a chance to live no matter how short their lives, but females, ordinary, ungifted ones, just get soft and die. (184)

Louise sees herself as one of the ordinary, ungifted ones. So instead of getting soft and dying, she has made her shell. The process of unmaking it is a long and painful business for her as well.

That process begins when she leaves the island, but it just begins. It continues when she refuses to give in to the medical establishment, to be given a life. Instead, she chooses again. The process continues as she chooses Appalachia, as she chooses to marry, as she chooses a family, as she chooses to have her mother come to live with her. It is well on its way when she holds the twin and nurses it at her own breast. No good oyster here.

But in displaying Louise's freedom and power to choose, Paterson also presents the reader with an almost fearful paradox. Though she chooses her own life, it seems that that choice has been formed for many years. Her choice is a mixture of freedom and all the forces that have been shaping her during her life on Rass. When she first meets the man who will be her husband, this tension is made explicit: "'I kept wondering ever since you came. Why would a woman like you, who could have anything she wanted, come to a place like this? Now I understand. . . . God in heaven,'—I thought at first it was an oath, it had been so long since I'd heard the expression used in any other way—'God in heaven's been raising you for this valley from the day you were born.'" (236). At first infuriated, Louise falls in love with him when he smiles. She will not react to his observation until the novel's conclusion, where the Calvinist paradox seems for a moment to become clear. Her freedom, and the ways God has been preparing her from the day she was born, are all one thing. The sounds of the marsh, the honking of the geese, the wind off the bay—all this was preparing her. But the singing of her father, the grace of her mother, even the shell she had to break—all this was preparing her as well. It is a matter of great wonder to her, as she walks back home through the snow. She has been prepared, like Jess and Gilly, to choose hope and joy. And, like Jess and Gilly, she finds it. Slowly and painfully, she finds it.

4.

Exploring the Boundaries of the Family

In the *Great Gilly Hopkins* Paterson examines a child desperately in search of the family, an outcast from another family. In *Jacob Have I Loved* Paterson focuses on an adolescent who alienates herself from her family, who becomes a prodigal child through her own choices, as, of course, all prodigals do. But *Jacob Have I Loved,* like *Bridge to Terabithia,* also examines the life of a family, searching for ways by which the nature of a family might be defined.

Paterson's next three novels—*Come Sing, Jimmy Jo, Park's Quest,* and *Lyddie*—all give center stage to the question of how a family might be defined. In each case Paterson explores the question by looking at those things that bind a family. Each of the families in these novels is losing or has lost its cohesion, and Paterson charts three very different courses that the child protagonist takes in the face of the potential loss of the family. The repeated line in *Lyddie*—"We can stil hop"—is in some ways the culmination of this grouping of novels, for each of the characters comes to the same conclusion—a conclusion to which other Paterson characters have also come.

Come Sing, Jimmy Jo

Come Sing, Jimmy Jo (1985) is about the gift, represented in this novel by the gift of singing. When young James finds that he indeed has the gift, he is thrust into a limelight he had always hoped to avoid. What had been so private is ripped into the public glare, and suddenly James is faced with all sorts of complexities he had never anticipated. Is fulfilling his gift worth leaving home and his grandmother behind? Is it worth the tensions created between James and his mother? Is it worth the breakup of his family? Is it worth the terrible discovery that his father may not be his biological father? In short, is the gift such a terrible master that he must fulfill its calling, despite the pain? Paterson does not give an easy answer to these questions.

The novel opens with Grandma smoking a pipe, listening to James play his guitar and sing on the porch of their mountain home. James's family—which consists of his grandparents, his parents, and Uncle Earl—are all from a singing tradition, and the rest of them—called, simply, the Family—are off on tour. When they return, carrying all their fussing and arguing with them, they bring news of a manager who soon appears and suggests what no one had imagined: that James become a part of the act. Olive, James's mother, is appalled. Insecure and unsettled, she needs to feel that she is at the center of things, and James threatens that centrality.

With the support of Jerry Lee, his father, James is able to conquer his fear and make it through his first concert. But very soon things begin to change, and he is converted into Jimmy Jo. As the Family achieves more success, James realizes that he is being made over into some creature the public will cherish; he also begins to realize not only how important success has become to his mother, but how that success seems to be more important to her than he is. The only constants in his life seem to be his grandmother and his father, Jerry Lee.

When the Family moves to Tidewater, Virginia, to take up a six-month contract with a television show, "Country Time," James finds that his world is truly being remade. He is cut off from his grandmother and thrown into a new school, where he, like Jess Aarons before him, only wants to be average enough so as not to stick out. To do this, he tries to hide his identity as Jimmy Jo. Here he is befriended by Eleazer Jones, a student who is constantly in trouble but who seems to find in James a kindred spirit, as indeed they are, despite enormous differences.

The show goes well for the Family, so that Keri Sue (the name Olive has taken on) does not seem to notice the tensions under which her son labors. In creating an image that will please the fans, she manipulates him into being Jimmy Jo, though at the same time her jealousy increases. James's only connections to his real self are his grandmother and Jerry Lee, but even these connections are threatened. His grandmother is far away, and a stranger, Flem Keeser, has appeared, suggesting that he is Jimmy Jo's true father. It is a suggestion that James at first dismisses, but, putting this together with other clues from absorbed conversations, he begins to suspect it is the truth.

Other tensions begin to mount. Keri Sue and Earl are changing, both personally and professionally. While Jerry Lee is gone to check on his mother, James discovers Earl and Keri Sue in a compromising situation. They also agree on a more Nashville-oriented sound—something that will advance Earl's and Keri Sue's careers though it would hurt the career of the Family as a group. This becomes especially difficult when Keri Sue sets James up for an interview that will reveal his identity to his classmates, and, most poignantly, when she and Earl steal a song that Jerry Lee had written expressly for James.

When the family returns to the mountains for Christmas, Jerry Lee finds out about the song, but while James wants him to confront Keri Sue and Earl, Jerry Lee resists. He is unwilling to destroy the ties of the family. James withdraws. He will no longer sing with the group; he talks to no one but Eleazer. Things turn around when James finally confronts his biological father. He realizes that no matter how tough things get, a father does not run off. In that sense, Jerry Lee is his true father, and the Family is his true family. Like Jerry Lee, he discovers the importance—and permanence—of family ties. That night in a concert, he sings "Let the Circle Be Unbroken" and resolves that he will not be the one to break it.

The novel's opening, in which James sings for his grandmother, is emblematic of those ties that bind the family. It is music that keeps the circle unbroken, that gives the family its sense of purpose, that even provides it its history. It is music that stills the squabbles. When James's grandmother weeps at his singing about a mother waiting in glory "just for me," James interprets her crying as sorrow over her own mother. But he is quite wrong; it is the sheer beauty of the music that moves her.

When the Family first returns home, they have a typical squabble, and a cold silence ensues. Jerry Lee, almost without thought, begins to strum his banjo, and instantly James recognizes the wisdom of his father. Music brings a kind of healing. Soon they are both playing, "and they both turned and sang for Grandma, who knocked the ashes out of her pipe so she could give herself over to weeping with pure and free delight."[1] This is what music can do for the family, and in the end James hopes that the public image that they convey of a close family singing group will indeed become a private reality. In short, he yearns for the Family to be a family. The novel ends with the hope, though not the certainty, of this prospect.

Set against the binding powers of music are the ambitions of Keri Sue and Earl to use music—perhaps even to use Jimmy Jo's gift—to enter an entirely different world, a world not so much of money as of adoration. Keri Sue wants James to play a part, to act as a member of a family that really does not exist except in the minds of the "Country Time" fans. The result is a rejection of, and perhaps even scorn for, her old world.

As Earl seems to accept her new reality, he, too, becomes an element threatening the family's unity. He sees her as a star rising beyond the world he had once accepted, and he allies himself with her. (This is hardly difficult for him, for he is attracted to her sexually as well—another threatening element.) Both Earl and Keri Sue want to abandon the old styles of music, which in fact means abandoning James's grandparents.

Beneath all of those tensions are unspoken ones. Keri Sue is almost maniacally jealous of James's talents and clearly sees him as a rival for the affection of the fans. Her schemes to minimize his involvement in the performances of the Family are transparent even to him. And beneath this tension lies the mystery of James's birth. Keri Sue fears the revelation of his true parentage, not only because of the tensions it will create within the family, but—again unspoken—what the revelations would do to her image.

James is aware of all of the tensions, which are exacerbated whenever the family is not singing. Early in the novel he cannot understand why his family is so torn. Later he cannot understand why Jerry Lee is unable to confront the threatening tensions head on. His response is at first to connect with his grandmother. (Perhaps his sense of these tensions is also part of his unwillingness to sing in public.) Later, when he is taken away from her by his family's singing commitment, he draws closer to his father, who, with his grandfather, seems to be the only one not caught up in the Family's success. Later still, when his relationship with Jerry Lee is threatened by the revelation of James's true birth, James retreats into isolation and silence, which is broken only by the appearance of his grandmother, who reaffirms the ties of the family. And with her appearance and that reaffirmation, James begins to see things in a new way: "His circle was here: Grandma and Grandpa, standing where he had left them just off stage; foolish Keri Sue, who did need him and Jerry Lee to take care of her—did it hurt her that he had always loved Grandma and Jerry Lee instead of her, his own momma?—poor old Earl acting so big, but really scared that he, too, was outside the circle; and Jerry Lee" (178). In the music James finds a way to express his love for and commitment to the circle, and as he sings he comes to new understandings. He sees that the tensions that threaten the family all come out of their emotional needs—needs too deep to be expressed or even to be consciously admitted.

For James, the conscious moment of growth comes when he faces the truth of his parentage. Having descended into the hell of feeling that he does not belong anywhere, he confronts Flem Keeser, his biological father. Keeser comes dressed in his navy blues, and James, growing more attuned to people's foibles, realizes that Keeser is both nervous and anxious to impress. But James will not be impressed. When Keeser greets him as "Jimmy Jo," James asserts the reality of his own world, rather than the "Country Time" world, by correcting him to "James."

James's moment of crisis comes when he allows for Keeser's biological claim but rejects his claim of real parenthood: "I guess in a matter of speaking I am your son. But"—he took a deep breath—"you ain't my daddy" (176). This, he asserts, is because Keeser abandoned Olive when she became pregnant. But the deeper rejection comes out of James's awareness that a father is much more than a biological parent—the same truth that Muna learns in the *The Sign of the Chrysanthemum.* A father is one who loves, who abides by commitments, who holds the circle together. It is, of course, Jerry Lee. Thus when his grandmother comes to bring him to his family, James comes gladly and focuses on Jerry Lee: "Oh, Jerry Lee, I done you wrong. You was trying so hard to hold us all together. I nearly broke it. Maybe it can't be held together. Maybe you're a fool to try, but I swear, Daddy, I ain't going to be the one to break it. On the Bible, I swear it" (178). After his moment with Keeser, James had suggested to himself, "I done it. I growed up" (177). He has indeed growed up. He has come to new awarenesses and new commitments. He is truly Jerry Lee's son, resolved to hold the circle together with love.

Similarly, he is truly his grandmother's grandson, though there is no biological connection. In the words of one of the songs James sings, she is "precious and worn," and James's greatest pain is his movement away from her. She is, in fact, the part of his mountain world that is most dear, most real, most stable. And for her, James is himself a gift. He came into her life just when her voice had given out: "Afterward you was with me. It all worked out" (84). The simplicity of that line—"It all worked out"—belies the enormity of the impulses behind it.

Grandma is a literary descendent of Trotter and of Fusa. There is an ampleness to her that speaks of love. Like Trotter, she shows her love through food and through giving of herself. Her trip to Tidewater rescues James from the isolation he had imposed on himself. But also like Trotter, Grandma is a dispenser of wisdom, whether it be in her advice to James to give Jerry Lee a good Thanksgiving, in her refusal to admit that Olive displaced her in the Family (thus forcing James to choose between his mother and grandmother), or in her folk wisdom. When James asks her what he should do with his gift, she answers another deeper question: "Nothin's ever pure, James. Joy and pain always show up in the same wrapper" (84). This is, of course, what James finds out through experience.

When James hears that his name is being changed—and with it, his world—it is his grandmother who tries to comfort him: "Jimmy Jo Johnson. It's just a brand label. . . . You're really James. That ain't gonna change" (24–25). This, too, is a lesson James must learn, though for a time it seems to him that it will be difficult to hold onto himself. It is the memory of his grandmother that helps, particularly when he sings directly to her over the television airwaves. This is what connects him to his past: "Only when he was actually singing and picking did he feel right. He was with Grandma then, singing on the porch, looking down over the yard at the hog pen and Rosie's shed with the hen-house on the side, and looking up over the ripple of hills that rolled like waves to the higher Appalachians in the misty west. It was the music that tied him to home, to being James" (55).

Perhaps it might be expected that James's grandmother would serve as an anchor for James, but another very unexpected character plays a similar role: Eleazer Jones. On one level he is everything that James is not: he sticks out in a classroom, he openly challenges authority, he has a court of followers, he is physically imposing. And yet there is something in James that attracts Eleazer. Perhaps he senses James's struggle over his conflicting worlds, for Eleazer himself has such a struggle. At school he is the king, in control, but after school he returns to a broken home, with no father. The two bond, as Eleazer becomes protective, perhaps providing for James what he had never had. He gives to James true concern: "You be awright, white mite?" (159).

It is Eleazer who provides a moment of calm in James's tortured world. He does this by opening up his own world to James as he rows him out into the bay:

> It was like a dream—like being in another world. The sun was climbing high, and James forgot to be either cold or afraid. It was going to be one of those strange winter days when the temperature climbs almost to seventy and you're lulled into thinking that spring has come. He closed his eyes and bent his head back, feeling the warmth on his face. The sound of the water against the side was like music. He was safe, suspended in a magic world far away from both home and school. (166)

Both home and school are troubled places for James, but here Eleazer has brought him to a place apart, a place away from his own troubled home. He has shared his world with James.

Eleazer, too, is a dispenser of wisdom. He understands instinctly that a father is not someone who is absent from a son's life; he knows the principle. When James fears that a stranger's claims may indeed be true, Eleazer points out what is to him quite obvious: "Ain't you already got a daddy? . . . I seed you on TV. You got you a fine daddy. Plays a bad banjo. I think my mama gots a crush on him. . . . I know that's your daddy. . . . Multiple-choice daddies, and me, I don't even have one" (158–59). The joke is tinged with pain, but James begins to realize that he does indeed have a daddy, and that he has had one all along. Eleazer, together with James's grandmother, has prepared him for his resolve to keep the circle unbroken.

Like Jess, James is the special, gifted child who wants more than anything else normalcy. He wants his family to settle down and get along. He wants to be anonymous in school, and he works hard for the anonymity of the average. But at the same time he suffers from the demands of his gift. When his grandmother asks him if he wishes to stop singing on the stage, he says no; despite his fear and the oppressive fans, he finds a fierce joy in his performance. And his grandmother knows that the gift is given only to be given: "The Lord don't give private presents. . . . If he give you somethin', it's only because he thinks you got the sense to share it or give it away. You try to keep the gift to yourself, it's liable to rot" (23). When James suggests that the Lord has not spoken to him about this, his grandmother's response rings with finality: "He give you the gift, James. That's all he got to say" (23).

What James eventually realizes is that the gift must indeed be given, and it must be given sincerely, not merely performed. When he first encounters his audience, his lack of glasses makes him see them all as blurred melon heads. But later he realizes that they are people—sad, lonely, and needy people—as he himself is: "He wanted to reach out to them all and heal their hurts" (88). Later he revises his assessment: "How had he ever thought they were melons? They were so full of love, looking up at him . . . all full of hope for a present. And he had the gift" (178). These perceptions come perhaps more from James than from the audience, and perhaps each time he is describing his own family more than the audience. He may even be describing himself. In each case, however, he recognizes the gift as something to be given, something to heal and to bring love and hope.

But as his grandmother observes, pain and joy show up in the same wrapper. The gift brings pain before it brings healing and love. For James, the cost of the gift is not greater than the giving of the gift, even as the cost of remaining a family is not greater than the remaining.

"Everything dances," James once tells his friend Will Short (63). That basic assumption, held simply and without question, is a measure of James's ownership of the gift. The world moves in rhythm, a rhythm he feels. But in the declaration "Everything dances" James speaks of his own family, which has its own harmonies and rhythms. If James cannot keep these harmonies going, he can at least prevent his terrible and beatific gift from sundering them.

Park's Quest

George Woods, in an interview in one of the early issues of *Lion and the Unicorn,* railed against books that use a quest to structure plot situations. In his attack he pointed to the work of Susan Cooper: "She is a beautiful writer, but when you start reading the books, you find one damn quest after another. It's always the battle between good and evil, between the forces of light and dark—forever. As soon as the hero finishes one quest, he's given another one."[2] It might be argued that the fight of good against evil should indeed be endless, but that is not Woods's principal point; he instead argues against the quest motif.

This concern arises from the very title of Paterson's *Park's Quest* (1988), which is about a young boy in search of his father—and of his extended family. The use of "quest" suggests a traditional use of that motif, but "Park," short for Parkington Waddell Broughton V, seems to undermine the high seriousness of the notion of a quest. Park is indeed from a noble lineage, a distinguished military family. But his quest is not the one he imagines; nor is it not conducted in the great and noble way he had imagined, and the people he meets are not characters out of Thomas Malory's *Le Morte Darthur*. In his imagination he conducts the kind of quest Woods finds so objectionable, but at the same time he conducts another quest with real characters in a much different landscape. Only at the end of the novel do these two quests fuse.

The novel opens with Park yearning to know more about his father, who has died in Vietnam, and of his father's family. His mother is strangely reluctant to tell him anything, or even to take him to the Vietnam War Memorial to see his father's name. Park assumes that she believes he is too young, and he learns what he can about his father through his father's books, particularly the stories of Joseph Conrad. When he finally does visit the War Memorial—alone—he resolves that he must find out more about his father.

His mother reluctantly writes to the home of the Colonel, her father-in-law and Park's grandfather. Up until this time Park had not known that his grandfather was still alive. Park is invited to stay at the Colonel's farm and soon goes to see him. But he is sorely disappointed. His grandfather is an invalid who lives behind a closed bedroom door; his uncle, Frank, has married a Vietnamese woman (one of those who killed my father, thinks Park) who is now pregnant; he is fed and watched over by a somewhat silly housekeeper; and he is irritated by the taunts of Thanh, the daughter of Frank's wife.

Soon Park is not sure why he has come. He does not seem to fit into the life of the farm, nor has he even had the opportunity to see his grandfather. But he is eventually able to see beneath the surface of things as he begins to learn parts of his own story. He sees Thanh's pain and fear of being rejected. He sees Frank's natural goodness. Soon he is working with them both. But when he first sees his grandfather, he is terrified by his paralysis and the "Haaa" that comes from his throat, and he flees.

Park is horrified by the vision but stays, working in the garden with Thanh, learning to shoot with Frank. When Frank asks Park to watch over the Colonel in his wheelchair on the porch, Park fears a repetition of the "Haaa," but his grandfather is silent. Park falls asleep, and when he wakes, he is horrified to see that Thanh had dashed down the hill, pushing the wheelchair in front of her. At the bottom she gives the Colonel some of the cool spring water, and Park pushes him back, hurrying so that no one sees. His grandfather smiles, and Park is amazed at his response to this adventure.

Later Park shoots a crow accidentally, and Thanh, who has been shot at in Vietnam, attacks him, fueled by her fear that Frank will reject her after his own child is born. After she leaves Park finds that the crow is not dead, and, bundling it in his shirt, he carries it to the barn and goes in search of Thanh. In her room he finds a picture of Thanh, Frank's wife, and his own father. He discovers the truth: Thanh is his sister, and his mother divorced his father because of Thanh's mother. And Thanh realizes for the first time that she has a brother.

That night, they go together to feed the wounded crow, but they stop on the way and bring their grandfather out into the night. Here he repeats his "Haaa" after Thanh has left to check on the crow. And suddenly Park realizes that he is saying his name, and that he, too, misses and feels guilt for his son. Thanh returns to say that the crow has flown away, and together—grandfather and grandchildren—they drink the cool, sweet water of the well under the watchful gaze of "all who saw them"—an archangelic host, the cloud of witnesses around us all.

Like many of Paterson's novels, this one is filled with stories half-told or barely hinted at. Since Park himself is on a quest for understanding, the reader is held to his viewpoint, his discoveries. The result is that the reader's discoveries are also limited. The reader does not know what precisely the circumstances were that led Frank to bring Thanh's mother to the United States, or how he fell in love with her. The reader does not know—but can guess—why they live in a separate, small house. Thanh, Frank reveals, has been shot at, but Park does not pursue this story. Park never learns the circumstances of his father's death, how he met Thanh's mother, or why his father's family is so very estranged from his mother—or if the estrangement comes from the other direction. His quest is perhaps not as focused as he had imagined it would be.

Amidst all of his discoveries—about his extended family, the divorce, his sister—he makes one very large one: there is a general diffusion of guilt over his father's death. Park's mother feels that her inability to accept Thanh's mother led Park's father to return to Vietnam and to his death. Park's grandfather feels guilt over his son's death, though the reason is unclear. Perhaps he sees it as the outcome of the family's emphasis on the military. Perhaps, Park muses, Frank feels some guilt as the son who never went and therefore lived. And Park himself feels this guilt; even though he had just been born, he senses that he might somehow be responsible for his father's apparently unnecessary return to Vietnam. Part of the quest is not only to find his father's family but also to begin to confront and deal with the guilt that has festered for almost 12 years—as long as Park has been alive.

Park's Quest, like *The Great Gilly Hopkins* and *Jacob Have I Loved,* is a retelling of a mythic story, set in a modern context. Here Paterson retells the story of Perceval, the chief protagonist of the quest for the Holy Grail. The parallels are quite explicit, and they are accented by Park's imaginative reconstructions of the world around him, as the situations in which he finds himself are transformed into Arthurian contexts, with Park as the protagonist:

> "Faugh! You are no knight!" The lady cried in disgust. "You are naught but a kitchen scullion, smelling of garlic and grease. How dare you presume to be my champion? Dismount, fool, and

> stand aside, lest the Black Knight skewer you on his spear and roast you in the everlasting flames!"
> Bold Gareth heeded not the lady's jeers, but put his spear at rest and rode full gallop at the Black Knight's shield.[3]

Park is here simply drying dishes in the kitchen with his mother, but he takes on the role of Sir Gareth, who started his career as a knight in Arthur's kitchen. At this point he sees himself as a champion for his mother, but she is reluctant to have him be that. Park has used the courtly world to give expression—perhaps unconsciously—to his own situation, where his mother will not allow him to play roles in their lives that he yearns for. He is too young to be her champion. "Faugh!"

Perceval, like Park, is brought up by his mother alone—his father, in some versions, having been killed in a battle by a wound to his thigh. He is unaware of his connections to the world of Arthur's court; some versions put Perceval as the son of Pellinore, King of the Isles. His mother, having lost her husband, is openly antagonistic to that world and seeks to shield her son from it. In fact, Perceval knows nothing of the world beyond the edge of the forest in which they live. Nevertheless, Perceval—like Park—is fascinated by the world of knighthood after encountering a group of Arthur's knights. He decides to journey to the court of Arthur, leaving his mother desolate with grief.

He is, however, very unsure of himself in this world—naive, blundering, brash, and cheerful. He is warned by the Lord of Gornemant to curb his questions. Thus he controls his curiosity when confronted by the mysteries of the Holy Grail, so that he fails to ask the right question of the Fisher King: "Who is served by the Grail?" or "What ails you?" Because the appropriate question is not asked, the wounded Fisher King, the keeper of the Holy Grail, is not healed, and his land remains wasted and desolate. Perceval is later told by his cousin that he failed because of his abandonment of his mother, who died of sorrow when he left.

Having failed at this, Perceval goes on a quest to find the Grail Castle and to ask the right question. He resolves to shirk no suffering or danger until he finds the Grail. Though he will never achieve the Grail, in some versions he is able to find the Castle and ask the question that cures the Fisher King. (In Malory's *Le Morte Darthur* it is Galahad who cures the Fisher King, though Perceval is present.) In the version of Chrétien de Troyes, Perceval wanders for five years until he finds a hermit who reveals to him that his own sin caused him to be silent in the presence of the Grail, and that the Fisher King's father is the one whom the Grail serves. Here the story breaks off, the author leaving many questions unanswered. (Some of those are answered in *The Perlesvaus,* in which Perceval asks the right question and becomes the heir of the Fisher King, reigning in turn for seven years, and then being taken up to heaven along with the Grail.)

At the beginning of *Park's Quest,* Park is in a situation very similar to that of Perceval. His father, too, has been killed in battle, and his mother has cut him off from the world that drew out his father. He is as isolated in his apartment as Perceval is in his forest cottage. But though Park has no knights to introduce him to his father's world, he does have his father's books as well as the War Memorial. He, too, leaves his mother behind, perhaps as desolate as Perceval's mother, to find his father's world. In that world Park learns of his grandfather's despair and guilt, as Perceval learns that his father died out of grief for his two dead sons, Perceval's brothers, whose eyes were pecked out by ravens and crows. Park's Uncle Frank recalls Gornemant of Gohort, whose patient teaching and gentle wisdom are important in Perceval's growth. And Park's encounter with the crow (perhaps avenging Perceval's brothers) recalls Perceval's encounter with the falcon and wounded goose—an encounter that reintroduces Perceval to Arthur's court. It also recalls the opening of Chrétien de Troyes's romance, *Li Contes del Graal,* where Perceval first leaves his mother's cottage and enters "the forest, and his heart itself immediately rejoiced in the gentle season and the song he heard from the happy birds."[4]

Park is as brash and blundering as the young Perceval. He is unsure how he should behave at the Colonel's house, and he treats his Uncle Frank—at first—like a servant. He is almost comically naive. Like Perceval, he seems unaware of mysteries, such as the shrinelike spring house where Thanh uses the Grail/coconut to carry fresh water to refresh body and spirit. His grandfather is indeed the maimed Fisher King, consumed by guilt and impotence. Before Park had left home, he had questioned as frequently and as irritatingly as Perceval: "Can I do anything for you?" (12), he asks his mother who is sitting in a darkened room. "If he just knew the right question," he thinks, "the one that would unlock all the others—" (13), but he does not know the right question and in fact is warned against asking too many questions. The result is a terrified silence when he first meets the Fisher King. He does not ask the question that will unlock other questions, that will cure the Fisher King.

Park must learn, like Perceval, before he can come to the point that he can ask the right question. In learning about her past, he learns about the pain his mother has suffered and is still suffering, the effects of the distance his mother has put between Park and his father's side of the family, and the debilitating blame and guilt felt by so many. Now he can ask the Colonel the right question: "'Park. You mean Park. I'm Park, and you're Park. That's what you mean, right? . . . What is it? Do you miss him? Is that it? . . . What's the matter? Please tell me,' he begged. And now, looking into the eyes, he saw his mother's eyes and his own eyes, as in a mirror. So that was it. 'You think you killed him,' Park said. 'You think it's your fault'" (147–48). And with the correct questions come release, healing, and community. Park "put his arms around his grandfather's shoulders and held them tight while they both cried like lost three-year-olds returned at last to their mothers' arms" (148). And at that, the crow flies away freely.

Throughout the novel Park has used the imaginative world of knighthood and noble quests to make sense of his own situations. They are not, as they might seem at first, escapes but attempts to articulate imaginatively what he most wants, and even what he most fears. Kept in ignorance of his father by the silence of his mother, Park finds ways to imagine the barriers that lie between him and what he wants to know. Unwilling to actively blame his mother or to feel anger at her silence, he goes into fantasy to make sense of it. This is a process that would be familiar to all readers of Maurice Sendak, but it is a new technique in the work of Katherine Paterson.

When he learns of the existence of his grandfather, Park instantly imagines a courtly context that will fit with his earlier courtly imaginings:

> "Grandsire!"
>
> The old man looked up at the word. He was sitting on a circular bench under a spreading oak two hundred years old—planted by the first king of this noble line who, when he tended that tiny sapling, could never have dreamed of the scene taking place today.
>
> Leaning heavily on his staff, the old king rose slowly. "My child," he said, his voice quavering with emotion. "Can it really be? Thou at last returned from thy quest?"
>
> The young knight ran forward then, and when he got to where the old man stood, he stretched out his hand, but his elder ignored it, dropping his staff and throwing both arms around the strong young shoulders. "God is good," he said, the words choked with unshed tears—(37–38)

Behind this construction lie many of Park's concerns. He wishes to see himself as part of a larger line, to learn about his father's family. He is, however, separated from them, and the reunion—after a long absence—would be the fulfillment of a quest. He would, in some senses, be returning home. Park is still unsure of his reception, however; he hopes it will be welcoming, and so the proffered handshake is converted into an emotional hug. Here Park's fears and wishes are given a new form.

Part of what Park learns, however, is that his imaginative constructs are, in the end, constructs. When he first arrives at his grandfather's house, he hears from his uncle that his grandfather has had two strokes: "He didn't even try to hide his feelings, his disappointment. Another stroke? He had pictured his grandfather as a noble, white-haired warrior. He couldn't put him into a hospital bed" (43). Park's response is to once again ask the wrong question—"How old is he?" (43)—and consequently to lose hope that what he had imagined was anything close to reality.

This does not stop Park from continuing to use the courtly world as a way of understanding his own world, but from this point on the imaginings become less hopeful, perhaps darker. He sees himself as disgraced and his grandfather living under a curse. And as the enormous truth about his own past comes on him, it seems to crowd out his imaginings, as the quest that he had imagined takes directions he had never anticipated: instead of a father, he finds a sister.

Still, the significance of those imaginings is not lessened. The reader has also come to see Park's quest as mythic: a boy's search for his father and, perhaps even deeper, for knowledge and healing. At the conclusion of the story, Park's immediate situation fuses with the imaginative world of the quest: "Then they took the Holy Grail in their hands and drew away the cloth and drank of the Holy Wine. And it seemed to all who saw them that their faces shone with a light that was not of this world. And they were as one in the company of the Grail" (148). This comes not from Park's perspective but from that of the narrator, who has made this fusion between two worlds. The hollowed-out coconut from which they all drink the springwater—grandfather and grandchildren—has not symbolized the Holy Grail for Park, but here it appears as the reward for the right question. In turning to his grandfather and asking that question, Park has released the guilt and blame that have cursed them both, and so they fall into each other's arms—as Park had earlier imagined in quite a different way—"like lost three-year-olds returned at last to their mothers' arms" (148). Each has come to the point where articulation is the beginning of healing.

The three are together called "the company of the Grail," and this occurs at the first time that some kind of understanding has developed between them. Perhaps for the first time the Colonel has been understood; he has clearly not expressed his own guilt to anyone before. Park has overcome his fear of his grandfather, as well as the anger over his father's death that he has directed at Thanh. And Thanh, so fearful of being abandoned, lays down her fear of her big "bruzzah." They are all very much like those who come home gladly to a mother's arms. They have all come to the end of a quest. Or perhaps it would be more accurate to say that they have merged their quests into one, and are no longer so alone.

The fusion of Park's imaginative world with the reality he finds validates his way of understanding what he is about. It is a way of investing the ordinary with extraordinary meaning, of creating Terabithia out of ordinary pine woods. The coconut shell and the spring water are a communion between them—a solemn, serious, and beatific drinking. The narrator refers to "all who saw them," and it is not to characters in the world of the novel that the narrator refers. The heavenly witnesses that observe are out of the courtly world, but out of the real world as well.

The fusion of these two worlds is suggested by the epigraphs from Rosemary Sutcliff's *The Sword and the Circle* and Joel Swerdlow's "To Heal a Nation." Both passages speak of memory. The first suggests how the age of Arthur and Launcelot, though it would come to an end, would still be remembered: "We shall have made such a blaze, that men will remember us on the other side of the Dark." The second speaks of the Vietnam War Memorial, of how the names carved into the stone wall seem to be warm and alive. Swerdlow suggests that the response is to call up "faith in love and in life" and an understanding of "sacrifice and sorrow." Park's quest is a fusion of these two—a search for something that lies beyond the time of darkness, beyond death, beyond disillusionment, and beyond the breaking of a family, and a search for understanding of sacrifice, sorrow, love, and life. They—Park, Thanh, and their grandfather—find this as they drink from the Grail.

Lyddie

The New England Gazetteer, published by John Hayward in 1839, describes the city of Lowell, Massachusetts, as a kind of industrial paradise:

> Lowell is finely situated in regard to health: it is surrounded by pleasant hills and valleys, and seated on a rapid stream. We are enabled to state on good authority that 6 of the females out of 10 enjoy better health than before being employed in the

> mills, and that one half of the males derive the same advantage.
>
> Lowell is very handsomely located: it is laid out into wide streets; all the buildings are of recent construction, and in a style of neatness and elegance.
>
> With regard to the future prosperity of this interesting city, nothing need be said to those who know that it was founded, and is principally sustained, by the most eminent capitalists of Boston; a city renowned for its enterprize, wealth, and public spirit.
>
> To strangers we would say—visit it. It is a pleasant ride of about an hour from Boston, by the rail-road. Foreigners view Lowell with admiration; and every American who sees it feels proud that such a city exists on this side of the Atlantic.[5]

This is an extraordinarily optimistic description, as, in fact, most of the descriptions in the *Gazetteer* are. Here blooms good health, wide streets, and benevolent capitalists. But the world of Lowell that Katherine Paterson discovered as she looked from the perspective of the factory workers was quite different. Begun as a part of her participation in the Women's History Project celebrating the 1991 bicentennial of Vermont, *Lyddie* (1991) pictures Lowell in quite a different manner.

Here Lowell is a place of squalor, especially for the Irish immigrants. The streets may be wide, but there are curfews. The valleys may be pleasant, but they are filled with the soot and ash of the mills. The factory workers work unbearably long hours, finding that their pay is decreasing while the owners' expectations are increasing. It is a place where many of the workers, coming off New England farms, find lending libraries for the first time, but most are too tired to read. These visions, which Paterson gleaned from such works as Benita Eisler's *The Lowell Offering: Writings by New England Mill Women (1840–45)*[6] and Harriet Hanson Robinson's *Loom and Spindle; or Life among the Early Mill Girls,*[7] stand in stark contrast to John Hayward's description.

Lyddie is a work of historical fiction, not a nonfictive account of Lowell. At the center of these competing visions stands the title character, who goes to Lowell presumably to seek her fortune; in fact, she is searching for herself as someone cut adrift from her family. She is Gilly Hopkins watching a family slip away, Park Broughton looking for a father who is gone, Takiko struggling to find a way not to be a slave, Wang Lee searching for himself.

The story opens with Lyddie protecting her family from the bear that has broken into their log farmhouse in Vermont. Their father has abandoned them, and their mother has settled into a deep depression. So it is Lyddie, with the help of her brother Charlie, who gathers the family into the loft, safe from the bear. Though they survive this, it is the beginning of a series of difficulties. Convinced that the bear is a sign of the end of the world, Lyddie's mother bundles off with the two little ones to her sister and a colony of those awaiting the end of the world. Lyddie and Charlie stay in the cabin, but after a time their mother rents the land and apprentices Charlie to a factory and Lyddie to a coach house. Lyddie swears that she will return and pay off the debt on the farm. But as the days stretch into months, Lyddie realizes that her salary, sent to her mother, will never pay off the debt.

Charlie is taken up and virtually adopted by a family in town, and Lyddie feels a growing distance from her family. She resolves that she will not be a slave to circumstances, and travels back to visit her cabin. It has been occupied by Ezekial, an escaped slave hidden by the Stevens, a Quaker family and Lyddie's closest neighbors. She toys with the notion of turning him in and using the reward money for the debt, but soon she sees that she cannot make a slave of this man any more than she is willing to be a slave herself. She leaves her cabin in the faithful hands of Luke Stevens, whose affection she refuses to acknowledge, and returns to the coach house to find her mistress furious at her absence. Lyddie leaves, having decided to travel to Lowell to become a mill girl and earn the money that will pay off the debt. And so she travels even further away from her family.

In Lowell she is led to a boardinghouse and quickly becomes part of the routine, rooming with three other girls. When she is brought to the mills and given a place at a loom, she is overwhelmed by the dusty air, the heat, the complexity and speed of the work, and the sheer noise. But driven by the desire for money, she becomes the most efficient worker in the room, operating four looms. She is befriended by Diana, an advocate of the 10-hour rule and consequently labeled as a radical. Diana introduces her to a world of ideas she had never imagined, though Lyddie is so caught up in her need to pay off the debt that she hardly has time for ideas.

But she does have time for story, and during one tired evening one of her roommates introduces her to *Oliver Twist,* a book about another child trying to not allow circumstances to lead to slavery. (This Charles Dickens novel had been published in England just five years before the events of *Lyddie.*) Entranced, Lyddie copies out passages and teaches herself to read, even spending some of her hoarded money to buy a copy of *Oliver Twist.* This love of story provides a break from the horrible bleakness of her life, though she does not yet completely realize how bleak that life is.

Soon each member of her family seems to be moving away from her. Charlie, rejoicing in his new family and in the prospect of school and regular meals, grows distant. He no longer shares the dream of returning to their cabin in Vermont. Baby Agnes dies, and eventually Lyddie's mother is committed to an asylum, where she too dies. Lyddie's uncle sells the farm to pay the expenses, despite Lyddie's pleas. And yet, in all of this, Lyddie is given new life with the coming of Rachel, her younger sister. Here is someone from her own family who loves her absolutely, who nurses her through illness, and who shares, though in a smaller way, Lyddie's dream of a reconstructed family. But the poisonous air of Lowell is soon too much for Rachel, so when Charlie comes, offering a place for Rachel, Lyddie lets her go. It seems she has nothing at all left. She is a slave for no reason.

Lyddie befriends Bridget, an Irish immigrant who comes to the mills. She soon finds that Bridget and her family are worse off than she, and Lyddie gives them some of her precious money for medicine. Lyddie seems to despise her inability to reach out to others graciously, but she is able to save Bridget from a sexual attack by their supervisor. The result is that Lyddie is maligned, the story twisted, and Lyddie dismissed and blacklisted with the other mills. Lyddie leaves Lowell and returns to her cabin, which has been bought by the Stevens family. There she again meets Luke, who offers her himself. She suddenly realizes that she will come to love him, but she will not come to him as someone beaten. She resolves, almost without thought, to follow the dream of one of her roommates: to travel to Ohio and enroll in Oberlin College. Then she will come back, no longer a slave.

For Lyddie, the process of not being a slave involves the process of learning to decide her own fate. At the coach house, Lyddie soon recognizes that however much she may deny it, she is essentially a slave, working for nothing, with someone else determining her life. Perhaps she has even begun to realize that her life has always been this way. She has always worked for others, even when those others involved her family. She resolves to leave the coach house, although Triphena, a fellow servant, tries to dissuade her.

> "I'm free. She's set me free. I can do anything I want. I can go to Lowell and make real money to pay off the debt. . . ."
>
> "How can you get to Massachusetts? You've no money for coach fare."
>
> "I'll walk," she said proudly. "A person should walk to freedom."
>
> "A person's feet will get mighty sore," muttered Triphena.[8]

Even in this moment of apparent freedom, Lyddie is still a slave. She still is a slave to the debt her parents have left. But she has, perhaps for the first time, made a decision on her own about the direction of her life.

The fortitude to make this decision comes from an unlikely source: a fugitive slave. Ezekial makes her see that she, too, has been enslaved. She refuses to see herself this way, but as she explains her position to Ezekial, she realizes he is right. Her instant response is to affirm that she would never turn him in to claim a reward. And later she gives him what little money she has so that he can make his way to freedom. Certainly the Stevenses will provide him with funds, but this gift comes from deep within the heart, from one fugitive slave to another.

Triphena is right: freedom is a sore thing. And Lyddie is actually walking into another kind of servitude. When she reaches

Lowell she becomes a slave to the great Boston capitalists that John Hayward extolled. Her hours are decided for her, her work determined, even her life controlled. She is to eat at a certain time, go to bed at a certain time, go to Sunday services (this she resists). She is not to make certain friends. But all of this she enters into, ostensibly for the purpose of the debt. She does not resist the encroachments of the company. She does not resist when the mill demands more work for less pay. She is more a slave now than ever before.

When she arrives in Lowell, there is at least an ostensible reason for this servitude: she has a dream of gathering her family back together and returning to the farm. This dream seems as hopeless as her dream of having her father return. But it is the one thing that drives her on. She writes desperately to her mother asking how the debt is to be paid, but she receives no answer. When the farm is to be sold, her brother provides no help. In fact, Lyddie's story once she leaves the farm is one of increasing isolation. First her mother and the two youngest children leave; she never sees two of them again. Then Charlie is absorbed into a new family; he apparently sees little need to maintain the boundaries of their family. Lyddie is cast off by them just as she has been cast off by her father. She has, it seems, two moments of real happiness: when she lives with Charlie in the cabin, and when Rachel comes to live with her. But both episodes are fleeting, and both end with terrible sadness. When Charlie comes to take Rachel away, Lyddie knows that this may be the last time she ever sees him. She cannot say good-bye. She also knows that Rachel, brought safe and secure into a new family, may forget her as well: "Mrs. Phinney would keep her safe. She could go to school. She would have a good life, a real mother. And she will forget me, plain, rough, miserly Lyddie who only bought her ribbons because she was shamed to it. Will she ever know how much I loved her? How I would have gladly laid down my life and died for her? How, O Lord, I am dying this very minute for her?" (144–45). The movement, dramatic and unexpected, from the third person into the first person narrator suggests how deeply Lyddie feels this loss. It represents the loss of her dream. There is nothing more to work for other than work itself.

When all else is stripped from Lyddie—her parents, her siblings, her friends, her farm, her job—it seems that Lyddie has little recourse. In fact, however, at least some of that stripping down, particularly the loss of the job, is what allows Lyddie to move out of slavery. It seems that her only option as a single woman is to marry Luke Stevens, who has been presented as an enormously sympathetic character, the only character to remain completely faithful to Lyddie. And though the conclusion of the novel suggests that this will indeed happen, it does not happen yet. Lyddie resolves to become her own person, to decide for herself what she will become. She will go to Oberlin: "I won't come back weak and beaten down and because I have nowhere else to go. No, I will not be a slave, even to myself" (182). Here is the release. Lyddie has been a slave to herself, her own vision of what the family should look like, her own relentless demand that she must beat back circumstances, her own terror of committing wholeheartedly to someone outside her family. She releases her own demands, will travel to Oberlin to learn, and will come back out of her own choice to marry Luke.

Reviewers recognized the importance of Lyddie's fight for freedom, as well as her tenacity. Elizabeth S. Watson, reviewing in *Horn Book,* suggested that *Lyddie* was a "story of grit, determination, and personal growth," the first two qualities emphasizing Lyddie's spirit.[9] Natalie Babbitt, writing for the *New York Times Book Review,* noted that "Paterson's novels are all, in one way or another, celebrations of the resilience of the human spirit at war with adversity." Lyddie, Babbitt goes on to assert, must be larger than life to endure what she endures.[10] Certainly she is drawn with as large a capacity to endure as Trotter has to love.

Lyddie has imaged circumstances by recalling the bear breaking into the cabin. She resolves to always stare the bear down. Even the shuddering looms take on the image: "No matter how fast the machines speeded up, Lyddie was somehow able to keep pace. . . . It was almost as if they had exchanged natures, as though she had become the machine, perfectly tuned to the roaring, clattering beasts in her cave. Think of them as bears, she'd tell herself. Great, clumsy bears. You can face down bears" (97). In fact, all alone, she almost does. Lyddie has a strength reminiscent of Gilly's. Both are abandoned, and both use their tremendous strength to deal with that abandonment. But there is no Trotter for Lyddie, who must instead recognize the bears within herself on her own. Thus when she decides to enroll at Oberlin, she reasons out the decision using familiar language: "'Im off,' she said, and knew as she spoke what it was she was off to. To stare down the bear! The bear that she had thought all these years was outside herself, but now, truly, knew was in her own narrow spirit. She would stare down all the bears!" (181). Here is a moment of self-realization. What she had imagined as being outside was truly internal. She perhaps goes too far here; in fact, there are bears on the outside and she has stared down a few. But she only now comes to recognize that she must see herself as being free before she is free.

In addition, Lyddie must see that being free does not mean being without entanglements. She does not fill the loss of her family with the gaining of close friends. Diana and Bridget remain set apart, always kept at a distance; eventually the bears remove them from the circle of Lyddie's life. She has resisted the love offered by Luke because she sees in it further entanglement, and thus a further opportunity of being abandoned, left behind. This is what she first thinks when she suddenly realizes that she could love Luke: "Tarnation, Lyddie Worthen! Ain't you learned nothing? Don't you know better than to tie yourself to some other living soul? You'd only be asking for trouble and grief. Might as well just throw open the cabin door full wide and invite that black bear right onto the hearth" (181). And this is in fact what she does; like Jess, Gilly, and Park, she throws open the cabin door and dares new relationships. And with the daring comes the establishment of a new family.

Triphena refers to Lyddie as a frog in a butter churn, who kicks and kicks and kicks until the milk turns to butter and he is saved from drowning. "Some folks are natural born kickers. They can always find a way to turn disaster into butter," Triphena suggests (28). Lyddie's response is a silent one: "We can stil hop" (28), quoting a letter her mother had written after leaving the cabin. Her mother had written it to suggest that she was still hoping for the end of the world—a self-destructive impulse coming out of her depression. (She too has been abandoned.) But Lyddie and Charlie have made that impulse into a joke to affirm their struggle to survive. Again and again, as Lyddie seems to be moving farther and farther into an inescapable hole, she remembers the line "We can stil hop." (There is a temptation to see in the misspelling a pun on Triphena's frog story, but certainly Lyddie does not see this connection.)

The quote concludes the novel, suggesting a truly happy ending, perhaps the most happy ending since that of Takiko and Goro, who carry the pain of their past but are also able to live fully in the joy of their new family. It also connects *Lyddie* to all of Paterson's work, and to her large theme: the need for hope. Lyddie hopes for something to, in D. H. Lawrence's words (though not his meaning), relieve her of the burden of being herself, so that she may be more truly herself. Although there seems little reason for continuing this hope through the course of the novel (this may be the closest Paterson has ever come to writing a novel like those of Robert Cormier), in the end it is fulfilled.

Lyddie's search for her family, her dream, her staring down of bears, her ability to "stil hop" are all played against the background of two principle settings: the Vermont mountains and the industrial city of Lowell. There is almost a sense here of the medieval stage. The farm in Vermont is certainly no paradise, but it stands as virtually a spiritual goal for Lyddie. After the departure of their mother, Lyddie and her brother grow close as they work the farm. They endure poor food, surviving on barks and what they can hunt, but shared hardship breeds closeness. When the calf is born there is "great rejoicing and a new abundance of milk and cream" (8). They gather sap for maple syrup, learning all the time to become successful farmers. Despite the difficulties, the setting is idyllic:

> The late May sky was brilliant dare-you-to-wink blue, and the cheek of the hillside wore a three-day growth of green. High in one of the apple trees a bluebird warbled his full spring song, chera, weera, wee-it, cheerily-cheerily. Lyddie's own spirit rose in reply. Her rough hands were stretched to grasp the satin-

> smooth wooden shafts of the old plow. With Charles at the horse's head, they urged and pushed the heavy metal blade through the rocky earth. The plow cast up the clean, damp smell of new turned soil. Cheerily-cheerily. (8)

The images here are fertile and full: the green hills, the blue sky, the damp smell of the earth. It is not Eden; the ground is rocky and hard to plow. But there is the goodness of doing one's own work for one's own livelihood.

Lowell is a dramatic contrast, especially when considered against the green hills and blue skies. The first sight of the city recalls the bear to Lyddie: "[The buildings] were huge and forboding in the gray light of afternoon. She would not have believed that the world contained as much brick as there was in a single building here. They were giants—five and six stories high and as long as the length of a large pasture. Chimneys, belching smoke, reached to the low hanging sky" (51). This passage recalls Charles Dickens's description of Coketown in *Hard Times:* "a town of red brick, or of brick that would have been red if the smoke and ashes had allowed it. . . . It was a town of machinery and tall chimneys, out of which interminable serpents of smoke trailed themselves for ever and ever, and never got uncoiled."[11] The menacing air of Coketown, the foul factories, the grasping owners, and the degraded workers all recall the situation of Lowell, experiencing its own industrial revolution. Lyddie turns away from it to the world of a novel just as Sissy Jupe escapes from fact to fancy.

It is natural for Lyddie, a farm girl, to compare the brick buildings to a pasture. But the contrast is a stark one. The solid brick buildings will hold her away from pastures, so that she will not even see the smoky sky that infects the lungs of her roommate Betsy and later her sister Rachel. The mill itself is a place of noise: "Clatter and clack, great shuddering moans, groans, creaks, and rattles. The shrieks and whistles of huge leather belts on wheels. . . . A factory was a hundred stagecoaches all inside one's skull, banging their wheels against the bone" (62–63). Later, in the winter, Lyddie never even sees daylight: "Lyddie went to work in the icy darkness and returned again at night. . . . The brief noon break did not help. The sky was always oppressive and gray, and the smoke of thousands of chimneys hung low and menacing" (101). Lyddie's first reaction is predictable: "Her impulse is to turn and run to the door . . . out of this hellish city and back, back, back to the green hills and quiet pastures" (63). This is in fact the direction she will eventually take, but she will turn to the green hills only after Oberlin, only out of her own choosing, just as Louise chooses Truitt and her life.

Lyddie represents one more variation on Paterson's theme of hope—a variation that would be familiar to any reader of John Steinbeck's *East of Eden*: hope comes out of choice. Lyddie's hope seems forlorn and almost pointless until the final scene, where she can choose a life and a partner. In fact, she chooses to affirm both herself and the beginning of a new family.

Each of the three late novels where Paterson focuses on the boundaries of a family—*Come Sing, Jimmy Jo, Park's Quest,* and *Lyddie*—conclude on this same note: the formation and affirmation of a family. For James, this is represented by an affirmation of those family members he already has. For Park, it is a recognition of family members he had never known. For Lyddie, it is a recognition of real loss (though she does stop to say farewell to Charlie and Rachel on her way to Ohio) and real gain. For each the hope finds real fulfillment while not negating the persistent pain of the past.

5.

New Directions and Old Forms

In 1981 Katherine Paterson translated "The Crane Wife," a Japanese folk tale that had been retold by Sumiko Yagawa. This was in some ways a return to those arenas she had frequented in her historical fiction. And yet it was a new direction, both in terms of the use of folklore and the act of translation. In fact, the next decade would show a multitude of new directions: another translated folk tale, a retold folk tale, an original "folk tale," a recast devotional work, a history of Asia in the year 1492, a controlled vocabulary book.

What is astonishing here is not simply the wide variety of forms; it is also Paterson's ability to convey those themes she had always played in so many different variations. Over and again she focuses on the nature of hope, on family, on prodigals lost and prodigals found.

The Crane Wife

One of the most popular of Japanese folk tales, "The Crane Wife" tells the story of the simple peasant named Yohei. He comes on a wounded crane in a snowstorm, and tenderly he cares for it. That night a beautiful and mysterious woman arrives at his home, offering to become his wife. They are extraordinarily happy. But one day the money that Yohei saves begins to run out, so his young wife weaves a mysterious cloth behind closed doors. Yohei is not allowed to watch, and when she emerges she is pale and thin. Yohei sells this cloth for a large sum and lives more comfortably than before.

But soon even this money is gone, and Yohei begins to want more wealth. His wife weaves a second time, assuring the farmer that this will be the last time she can perform the task. Paler and thinner than ever, she gives him another cloth to sell. But now Yohei is growing enamored of his wealth, and spurred on by a neighbor's acquisitiveness, he urges his wife to weave yet a third time. To this she reluctantly agrees, enjoining him not to look behind the closed doors.

But Yohei is unable to overcome his curiosity. When he does peer into the room, there is the crane, bloodied, plucking its own feathers out. He swoons, and when he awakens he finds another bolt of cloth, even more beautiful than the first two. But he also hears a distant voice bidding him farewell. "It was nearly spring, and, over the crest of the distant mountains, he could barely discern the tiny form of a single crane, flying farther and farther away."[1]

The text of Paterson's 1981 translation is marked by the simplicity and directness of the folk tale:

> Without stopping to eat or drink, the young woman went on weaving and weaving. Finally, on the fourth day, she came out. To Yohei she seemed strangely thin and completely exhausted as, without a word, she held out to him a bolt of material.
>
> And such exquisite cloth it was!

The voice here is straightforward, reporting action quickly and simply. The narrative voice refrains from commentary, choosing instead to let the characters establish a commentary themselves. The reference to the exquisite cloth seems to come from Yohei, not the narrator, for this is certainly Yohei's perspective. Though the narrative voice is only occasionally oral (as, for example, when it calls for the sounds of the crane—"basa basa"—or the loon—"tonkara tonkara"), it does capture a folk tale quality in its directness.

The story itself is not Paterson's, but some of the questions it raises are typical of Paterson's work. There is the dichotomy between the simple and good versus the sophisticated and grasping, found in both *Of Nightingales That Weep* and *Rebels of the Heavenly Kingdom.* Here it is portrayed in the evolution of Yohei's character. There is also an examination of the bonds of a family, particularly self-giving, trust, and responding simply out of love. Similar questions appear particularly in *Jacob Have I Loved, Come Sing, Jimmy Jo,* and *Park's Quest.*

Finally, the ending is certainly one that would appeal to Paterson. There is a real ending, and a real pain, for the crane wife is gone. But she has left with a blessing—"I pray that your life will be long and that you will always be happy"—and she does not reproach him for the loss of his "gentle, simple heart." His despairing cry suggests a growth and repentance, and the narrator points out—almost intrusively, unless read in the context of Yohei's growth—that it is nearly spring. The potential of spring, reinforced by Suekichi Akaba's graceful illustration of children pointing to the crane, suggest a kind of hope that Paterson would not find distasteful.

The Tongue-cut Sparrow

Like "The Crane Wife," "The Tongue-cut Sparrow" is a popular Japanese tale. The motif of the greedy wife and charitable husband is itself popular worldwide. The story opens with the kindness of the old husband, who feeds the sparrow. But when the sparrow drinks the starch that the old wife was preparing for the laundry, she responds in anger, snipping the bird's tongue. The old husband resolves to apologize for this act, and journeys into the mountains to find the sparrow. He is met by a man washing oxen, who gives him directions only when he has worked hard to help wash the beasts. He is then met by a man with horses, and again washes them. Finally he arrives at the home of the sparrow, who greets him politely, feeds him, and then offers a gift: he may choose between a large and smaller wicker basket.

He chooses the smaller, and warned not to open it until he arrives home, he carries it away with the goodwill of the sparrow. At home, he and his wife find it to be loaded with riches. She grows greedy, and she too sets out into the mountains to find the home of the sparrow, not thinking that the act of cutting its tongue will affect her reception. She too meets the man with the oxen and horses, but she washes them only hastily (the illustrations show her pulling their tails). She finds the house, but is served only poor fare. She too is offered a choice of gifts, and the old wife decides on the larger basket. Her curiosity is such that she cannot wait until she arrives home, despite a warning, and when she opens it she releases an enormous toad and a snake. She runs all the way home, barely escaping alive. "And from that time on, the old woman was cured of greediness, so they say."[2]

Paterson's 1987 version of the tale is somewhat simplified from the better-known version in which it is a neighbor who cuts the tongue of the sparrow and the old couple goes off together to find the sparrow. There the couple is mutually rewarded for their goodness; here the old woman will presumably share some of her husband's wealth, perhaps appropriately since she herself has repented—though the final phrase of the book ("so they say") leaves her repentance somewhat ambiguous.

Like many Paterson novels, this story leaves unanswered questions. Has the old woman reformed? Who are the men washing the beasts and what is their relationship to the sparrow? Is the old woman punished for greed (in choosing the bigger box), for curiosity (in not waiting until she reaches home to open it), or for her attack on the sparrow? Do the repeated requests for washing relate to the starch for the laundry? What will her relationship be to her suddenly wealthy husband? But folk tales do not answer questions like these, focusing instead on the central issue of the plot situation.

The characters of the old man and old woman are not outside the boundaries of Paterson's earlier work, though they are, as folk tale characters, much more one-dimensioned than Paterson's characters. They each act abruptly and impulsively. For the old husband, it is as natural as a gray sky in Michigan to seek out the wounded bird; for the old wife, it is natural to respond with greed and falseness. The one is affirmed, the other punished; Fukuji affirmed, Takanobu left in isolation; Goro affirmed, Hideo abandoned to a life of superficiality. The patterns are the same.

Paterson's translation is, like that of "The Crane Wife," highly readable. It is filled with Japanese onomatopoeic words that contribute to the Japanese feel of the text. The scissors snip: "chokin." The sparrow flies away home: "chun chun." The old husband washes the oxen: "binga binga." This is not a new technique; Verna Aardema has used it repeatedly in her retellings of folk tales. Here it adds an aural quality to the reading, which captures, as do the illustrations, the tale's culture. In addition, the sounds differentiate the old husband and the old wife. When she hastily scrubs the oxen, the sound is not the pleasing "binga binga" but a harsh and grating "kocho kocho" and "gosho gosho." Later the sounds of the snake—"suru suru"—and toad—"yota yota," "futt"—will be similarly harsh and threatening, yielding the final sound of the text, the old wife's wail: "Hi-yaaaa!"

The Tale of the Mandarin Ducks

The opening of "The Tale of the Mandarin Ducks" is as simple and as evocative as any in folklore: "Long ago and far away in the land of the Rising Sun, there lived together a pair of mandarin ducks."[3] Like most folk tales, this one brings a reader instantly to a remote, indeterminable time ("long ago") and to a distant and exotic place ("far away"). It is an out of the ordinary setting where out of the ordinary things can happen. And they do.

In this 1990 retelling Paterson sounds again the theme of hope, but there is an intense joy and beauty here that sounds much more fully than in her translations of *The Tongue-cut Sparrow* or *The Crane Wife.* There is much joy in the union of two lovers, who find each other in the most dreadful of circumstances where, it

From *The Tale of the Mandarin Ducks* by Katherine Paterson, pictures by Leo and Diane Dillon. Copyright © 1990 by Leo and Diane Dillon, pictures. Used by permission of Lodestar Books, an affiliate of Dutton Children's Books, a division of Penguin USA Inc.

seems, there should be no hope. Added to this is the traditional folk tale motif of goodness and generosity being rewarded. If Katherine Paterson's readers were still looking for the conventionally happy ending, here it would be.

The story begins in domesticity: the duck is sitting on her nest of eggs, while the drake has flown down to a pond to search for food. A hunting party led by the lord of the district sees the drake, admires his beautiful plumage, and determines to capture the bird. This his men do, despite the protestations of the samuri Shozo, who had been wounded and lost an eye in the service of a lord who now despises him for his lack of beauty. The lord takes the pet and displays him in a bamboo cage. But soon, as the drake thinks only of his lost mate, his feathers droop and lose their colors. He refuses to eat the food the gentle kitchen maid, Yasuko, brings him.

When the lord becomes angry at the drake's appearance, he refuses to follow Shozo's suggestion that the bird be released; instead he has it taken where he can no longer see it. Finally, Yasuko releases the bird one night into the darkness. The lord, furious at the thought that someone has taken something he owns, accuses Shozo of the theft, strips him of his rank, and makes him into a kitchen servant. Here he meets Yasuko, and the two fall in love.

When the lord hears of their happiness, he is angry and orders that they be drowned. But as his soldiers come to carry out the order, two messengers from the emperor, dressed in the colors of the ducks, arrive to lead the condemned to the Imperial Court. During the five-day journey to the court, the soldiers, frightened by the darkness, leave Yasuko and Shozo behind, and soon the two find themselves lost. But they are met by the two mysterious messengers, who bring them to a wood and grass hut. Baths are drawn, new kimonos brought, a feast set before them, and quilts laid out for them on the tatami floor.

In the morning Shozo and Yasuko awake to the smell of boiling rice; the messengers are nowhere to be seen, but on the path are two mandarin ducks, who seem to bow before they fly off over the highest trees in the forest. The story that began in domesticity ends in domesticity. Shozo and Yasuko live on in the cottage for many years, having many children, having learned that "trouble can always be borne when it is shared."

Originally meant as an anniversary present for her husband, John, this story of trouble shared and trouble borne focuses on the love between the two mandarin ducks and between Shozo and Yasuko. Paterson found the tale in Juliet Piggott's *Japanese Mythology,* which presents a much sparer version of the story while noting that the ducks were traditionally associated with happy marriages, certainly the case in this tale:

> The drake was caught and kept in a cage by a rich man, but was looked after by his manservant. The bird moped and would not eat. A serving girl in the household advised the manservant to release it, as it was clearly pining for its mate and would inevitably die in captivity. The owner of the mandarin duck was furious when he found the bird no longer in its cage and, suspecting the servant of having set it free, treated him with indifference verging on cruelty. The maid was much distressed by the abuse her fellow-servant was getting, for which she was partly responsible. Drawn together in this manner, the couple fell in love.

Piggott goes on to tell the fate of the couple. When the rich man hears of their love, he believes that they have jointly deprived him of his bird. He orders them executed. But just as they are about to be drowned, two messengers from the provincial governor arrive to announce that all offenders under sentence of death are to be sent to the governor. The servants are relieved, but also exhausted. During the long walk to the provincial capital they move more and more slowly, until they suddenly realize that the men they had been following had disappeared. Piggott continues,

> They spent the night in an old hut and when the lovers finally slept, the messengers appeared to each of them in a dream, saying they were the pair of mandarin ducks, the male of which they had enabled to rejoin its mate. On waking, the couple saw a pair of ducks by the entrance of the hut, which bowed their heads in greeting and then flew away together. The ser-

> vants naturally never returned to their master, but took employment in another district where they married. Their marriage was as close as that of the birds who had saved them from death in indebtedness for the preservation of their own union.[4]

Paterson has clearly changed and elaborated on a number of details here—as do all retellers of folk tales. The characters remain much the same, but in Paterson's version the master of the house, the male servant, and the provincial governor are elevated to a lord of the district, a samurai warrior, and the emperor—all positions that North American children might more readily recognize. This elevation also emphasizes the humiliation of Shozo, for whereas the corresponding character in Piggott's version is always a servant, Shozo is ignominiously demoted in Paterson's tale, a larger fall. In addition, Paterson emphasizes Shozo's nobility by allowing him to assume all of the lord's wrath. Whereas the original folk tale has the male servant release the drake at the female servant's suggestion, here Shozo realizes that the drake should be released, but it is the serving girl, Yasuko, who actually releases the bird. Shozo, guiltless, never blames or reproaches her, even though there is no indication that he had even known her before the incident.

In her changes and adaptations Paterson focuses on love in adversity, on mutual self-sacrifice, on the glad bearing of another's burdens. In the kitchen they fall in love while working with each other. In the woods they support each other first in fear of the soldiers, then in fear of the woods and darkness, then in fear of being lost. The response on the part of the ducks is also much more tangible in Paterson's version: instead of appearing only in a dream, they prepare food and bedding and draw baths.

The conclusion of Paterson's tale stresses the sense of home. Instead of traveling to another place, Shozo and Yasuko remain in the hut, the place where their love, begun in adversity, is fulfilled in the gratitude of the mandarin ducks. Released from fear because of their own goodness, they establish a home. The conclusion—"trouble can always be borne when it is shared" (a conclusion applicable both to Yasuko and Shozo and the ducks)—is emphasized and enriched by the adaptations.

In this story of troubles borne, what Paterson emphasizes is hope through mutuality. The lord, a character who anticipates Raphael in *The King's Equal,* is, despite his many courtiers, very much alone. Though he is manipulated, there is no sense that he is loved. He loves only that which pleases his eye, though to call his possessive instinct love is perhaps a misnomer. He wants to own whatever is pleasing. When he sees the drake he has it captured on a whim. In satisfying his whim, he tears the drake from its mate and dooms it. When it pleases him no longer, he becomes even more distorted in his possessiveness: he will keep the drake even though it no longer pleases him.

Shozo, in terms of the lord's regard, is not unlike the drake. He had once been the lord's mightiest samurai, but now he "was no longer handsome to look upon." But the lord still uses him. When it seems that Shozo displeases, he will not release him but put him out of sight. Like Raphael, this is a lord whose insatiable grasping prohibits any love, any real companionship.

The drake and his mate stand in contrast to the lonely lord. The duck is pictured on a nest, warming at least two eggs. It is not clear if the separation that the lord causes leads to the loss of the ducklings, but they are never shown again, and one illustration pictures an empty nest. In any case the separation is clearly destructive, since it is the separation, and not simply the captivity, that causes the drake's distress. Once the drake is released, he and his mate are never again shown apart.

The same is true of Shozo and Yasuko. Shozo is first shown at a court where he is clearly ill at ease. Wanton cruelty, whim, and mischief seem to rule here. His demotion to a kitchen servant is in fact the very thing that brings him joy: he learns to love Yasuko. When she suggests that she should admit her theft of the drake, Shozo replies out of his growing love, "Why should two suffer for one crime?" Already there is a sense of mutuality here. They bear the burden of the act—for neither sees it truly as a crime—together. When the lord hears this, he responds in a way that seems irrational: he orders their execution as "an example to all who would resist my will." There is no reason for him to identify Yasuko as one who resists his will. In fact, his anger arises at his seeing what he cannot possibly own. Finding that he cannot take their love from them, he decides to destroy them.

Shozo and Yasuko's love enables them to endure the fear of execution. When they are alone in the woods, Shozo affirms their mutuality: "Stand as close as you can so that your shoulder touches mine. Then we will not lose each other in the darkness." It is a very practical line, for it is dark and they need to stay together. But the line is also emblematic of their relationship. In times of trouble they will stand together and not lose each other. Here is true mutuality, emphasized by the Dillons' illustrations that picture them as always close together, always touching.

In the woods, in a moment of despair, Yasuko laments her release of the drake. "It is not foolish," responds Shozo, "to show compassion for a fellow creature." Shozo says this in the abstract, but in fact that compassion will have immediate consequences. The two ducks, in the guise of the imperial messengers, rescue them. Underneath the larger theme of troubles mutually borne is this lovely strain of folk tale truth: goodness is rewarded. The ending suggests this, but not in the sense that many folk tales do. Shozo and Yasuko will live happily ever after not because all of their troubles are at an end, but because all of their troubles—and their joys—will be faced together.

The Smallest Cow in the World

As Paterson was turning to new genres, in 1991 she tried her hand at an "I Can Read" book, published by HarperCollins. An earlier version of the book had been published by the Vermont Migrant Education Program, and indeed the book is dedicated, both by Paterson and the illustrator, Jane Clark Brown, to the children of that program. In this format Paterson was faced with a new challenge: using a simple vocabulary and simple sentence structures, she wanted to tell the story of a young boy in a migrant lifestyle. Her ability to overcome the limitations of the format, and indeed to use those limitations in her telling, is one of the strengths of this short book.

Marvin Gates lives with his family on Brock's Dairy Farm. When Mr. Brock decides to retire and sell the farm, Marvin must leave with his family to find another farming job. This also means that he must leave Rosie, a cow his family had dubbed the meanest cow in the world. For Marvin, however, she had been the most beautiful cow in the world. But now she is gone.

At the new farm everyone seems to settle in but Marvin. His father works on the tractor, his mother plants a garden, and his sister, May, finds a new friend. But Marvin is terribly alone. He imagines that Rosie has returned as the smallest cow in the world, and "Rosie" scrawls over their trailer, pulls up his mother's flower garden, and pulls down May's books from her bookcase. When his family finds him, they realize that Rosie is quite real to Marvin. They make a stable for her so that she will no longer be mean, and Marvin spends the rest of the summer with his cow.

But when Marvin brings the cow to school, both he and his sister are ridiculed. May's friend insists that he is only showing the workings of a good imagination, but May is mortified. The family, however, suggests that Rosie is about to have a calf, so she will no longer be able to go to school. Marvin agrees, having received assurance from his family that the calf will never be separated from Rosie and that she will never be lonely.

If Maurice Sendak tended toward realism rather than fantasy, this is a story he might have told. Like Max of *Where the Wild Things Are,* Marvin orders his world through his imagination as he tries to deal with emotions perhaps too complicated for him to understand and fears too deep and awful to face frontally. He begins in an Edenic setting, enjoying his life on Brock's Dairy Farm and finding in the maligned cow a friend that responds to him. But as a child in a migrant farm family he seems to have no assurance that home will remain home, at least in a physical sense. He sees Rosie's calf taken from her, and then Rosie from him, and he comes to fear the awfulness of separation. Nothing seems secure in this world, nothing lasts.

His response is an imaginative one: he reinvents Rosie so that the cow can be with him. He negates the separation and establishes strong bonds—bonds so strong that he will not even break them when he must go to school. In fact, he will only break those bonds when the imagined Rosie is given back an imagined calf, when she is no longer threatened by loneliness and isolation.

And this assurance, in the end, is what Marvin is seeking. What is extraordinary is that he finds it in a loving family. They understand his fears. They understand why Rosie has come back. They understand Marvin's need to sense his belonging to a family. In the midst of moving about, there must be that assurance. So they give it:

> "Will you always like Rosie?" Marvin asked May.
> "Of course I will," May said. "I think she is the most beautiful cow in the world."
> "We all love Rosie," said Mom, and she gave him a kiss.
> "Will we take her with us if we have to move to another farm?" asked Marvin.
> "We will never leave her behind," said Dad, and he gave Marvin a hug.
> May said, "No matter how small she is or where she lives or if she's smart or dumb, Rosie will have Dad and Mom and you and me and the smallest calf in the world. She will never be lonely again."
> "That's good," said Marvin.
> And he was right.[5]

The physical and verbal emphasis on love dominates this passage. And though they are all speaking ostensibly of Rosie, they are all, of course, speaking of Marvin, who is brought into a family, who is assured that though physical homes may change, certainly the sense of home established by this family will never change.

And here Paterson is able to use simple sentence structures to support this point: "We all love Rosie" and "We will never leave her behind," say Marvin's parents. Their verbal simplicity carries assurance; it is as though this is obvious, and nothing more needs to be said. Even May's "She will never be lonely again" carries this assurance. It is self-evident. The one long sentence in the quoted passage comes from May, and it repeats some of what had come before. Though a complex sentence, it, too, is assuring in its inclusiveness; the main clause includes the entire family, as well as Rosie and the calf.

The final short sentence, the concluding line of the story, carries assurance as well: "And he was right." Twice in the story an episode had concluded with a similar sentence, but with a different sentiment: "But she was wrong" (27, 45). In each case May thought that Marvin had overcome the sense of separation the move had caused, but she was wrong. In each case she had tried to ease Marvin's fears by suggesting another separation, both from the actual and the imagined Rosie. But at the tale's conclusion Marvin's fears are eased not by accepting separation but by affirming unity.

So when Marvin responds "That's good," the narrator's "And he was right" is an affirmation that it is good that Rosie will never be lonely again, but it is equally an affirmation that the family unity is inherently good, that what has been emphasized is on some deep level good. Gilly, Lyddie, and Jimmy Jo would have agreed.

The King's Equal

In 1992 Paterson saw the publication of *The King's Equal* (1992). Having retold several folk tales, she had turned her hand to casting an original tale while using the motifs and plot situations of older folk lore. Jack Zipes, writing in the *New York Times Book Review,* argued that "the structure of the story and the incidents illustrated show how the form of an old-fashioned fairy tale can be persuasively modernized."[6] This tale combines contemporary issues with the wisdom of a European folk tale, which treats expected motifs in startling ways and pushes conventions to find new ways of expression.

Paterson had met the Russian illustrator Vladmir Vagin in 1989 at a symposium for Soviet-American children's literature, designed to promote world peace. (Paterson had already participated in a joint Soviet and American project by contributing a selection from *Park's Quest* to *Face to Face* [1990], a collection of Soviet and American stories published to benefit UNICEF.)[7] After seeing Vagin's work—he is best known for his illustrations of Russian folk tales—Paterson determined to try her hand at a modern folk tale for him to illustrate. *The King's Equal* is the result. And it became a good match, as, in the words of Jack Zipes's review, "the bright pastel tones of Mr. Vagin's pictures highlight the hope in Mrs. Paterson's text" (27).

The story begins with a change in reign. The good old king is dying, and though the people mourn for that, they are more preoccupied with the coming reign of the king's son, who is vain, arrogant, and grasping. The old king, sensing his peoples' fear, leaves his son Raphael this blessing: that he may not wear the king's crown until he marries a woman who is his equal. The prince is furious, for he is so arrogant that he cannot believe any woman could be his equal.

After the king's death the prince cruelly abuses his people. He closes the schools: "From now on, I am doing the thinking for this country."[8] He collects all the gold and silver. He gathers all the livestock, grain, and vegetables, which he then sells back to his people. But though he grows richer and richer, he is not happy, for he cannot wear his father's crown. He sends his councilors to find his equal, but their searches are in vain, for he will never admit that anyone is his equal.

Meanwhile, in a distant corner of the kingdom, Rosamund is sent by her father up into the mountains, taking with her their three goats to protect them from the prince's agents. There she stops a wolf from taking one of the goats. But she finds that this wolf, who can speak, is actually a friend come to help her. At first he keeps her from starving, but then he reveals to her that her mother's blessing—mirroring that of the old king—is that she would be a king's equal. He sends her down to the palace wearing a gold circlet, for, he says, "the circlet of a friend is always magic" (34).

When she arrives, the prince finds her to be more beautiful than anyone he has ever seen. When she reveals to him that she knows he is lonely, he recognizes that she is more intelligent than he could have imagined. When she shows him that she is wealthier than he "for there is nothing I desire that I do not already possess" (44), he is convinced that this should be his queen. But she refuses, for, as she points out, she is more than his equal. She will marry him only if he spends a year up in the mountains caring for the goats. He reluctantly agrees, and she rules in his place, righting all of his wrongs: "The realm had never known such a cheerful, industrious, and kind ruler" (47).

In the meantime, Raphael learns humility and grace and cooperation in the small hut that he shares with the Wolf and goats. He is allowed to enter only when he comes to the point when he can ask to enter. There he learns how to bake bread, how to grind flour, and how to share and cooperate with another. He finds to his surprise that the animals become his friends. When he returns to the palace a year later, he has found humility and he has grown. No longer arrogant, and ashamed of the way he looks after a year in the mountains, he goes to the kitchen, where he hears the same songs that the Wolf had sung to him back in the hut. It is Rosamund, who recognizes how the prince has changed. When the prince turns to go, she calls him back. They are married that very night. And every winter, they return to the mountains, they and their children with them, to visit the Wolf.

When Raphael comes to Rosamund, he finds her in the kitchen baking. In the accompanying illustration her sleeves are rolled up and, as the narrator suggests, her face is "pink from the heat" (55). In the previous illustration of the prince it had been he at the stove, his sleeves rolled up, baking bread for his "family." In both cases Rosamund and Raphael are, in the prince's allusive words, making "daily bread" (62). There is a sense of rightness and proportion here. While once before Raphael had abused his people to gain wealth while producing nothing, now he has learned to provide and to find joy in that providing. And Rosamund, who had already known the lesson, has not forgotten it now that she is reigning. When Raphael finds her, she is alone in the kitchen, doing what brings fulfillment. Small wonder that the harvest has been great and that the land has prospered under her.

From Katherine Paterson, *The King's Equal.* Illustration by Vladimir Vagin. Copyright © 1992 by Vladimir Vagin. Used by permission of HarperCollins Publishers.

The Wolf is that strange, enigmatic figure out of folklore who seems to stand at the edge of action, who intrudes into the main action at times to propel motivations, and who then withdraws as peace, justice, and happiness are established. (In the central illustration of the book he stands outside the court on a wintry night, but clearly—and mysteriously—he is able to see the first meeting of Raphael and Rosamund, the meeting he had anticipated.) Like such figures, the Wolf seems to know more than he will ever tell; he seems to see a pattern that only he is able to perceive. He knows about the old king's blessing, but he also knows about Rosamund's mother's prophecy, that she would be a king's equal. He knows that Rosamund is the one who, in her goodness, will help her people, for she knows the lessons of friendship and love that Raphael does not. It is to her that the Wolf makes promises: her kindness and wisdom will not go unrewarded.

Both Rosamund and Raphael ask the same question of the Wolf: "Who are you?" The response is virtually identical: "'I am the Wolf,' the great beast answered. 'And someday I shall prove to be your friend'" (57). He will indeed prove to be so, principally by the lessons that he teaches and his encouragement to action. He will in fact not act for either Rosamund or Raphael; instead he will teach them the ways that they should act. Always he remains the Wolf, a simple yet enigmatic name that reveals little. Even in the illustrations he remains enigmatic, appearing in some almost comically domestic, in others as a fierce predator. If these were the *Narnia Chronicles,* Rosamund might well observe that he is not at all a tame wolf.

Like the *Narnia Chronicles, The King's Equal* expands on and plays with conventions of the fairy tale. Much here is familiar: the vain prince learning a hard lesson, the rewarding of innocence and virtue, the test as a way of growth, the search for a wise and beautiful princess, the guide with extraordinary powers, the humble lifted high. But Paterson crafts these motifs in unexpected ways.

The story turns on the first meeting of Raphael and Rosamund. In a conventional fairy tale, one might expect a Cinderella motif: Raphael falls in love with the beautiful princess of unknown (and humble) origins. He marries her and is transformed by her goodness. But instead it becomes clear that she will not marry him unless they are on equal terms. And though conventionally a reader might expect the female character to be attempting to prove her equality with the male character, with Rosamund it is exactly the other way around: "By your own words, my lord, you have declared me *more* than equal to you" (45). Raphael must measure up to Rosamund. By turning the convention around, Paterson has cast Raphael's testing into an entirely new context.

And by playing with these conventions, Paterson has emphasized the important themes in *The King's Equal*. As in the tales of *Angels and Other Strangers,* Paterson is pointing out the importance of right perception. It is not things that make one wealthy, nor, in fact, is it the lack of need that makes one wealthy, Henry David Thoreau notwithstanding. It is family and friends. At the end of the story Rosamund whispers, "A man who has friends is truly rich" (61). Raphael comes to learn this, suggesting, as in any good folk tale, that behind the story lies a tremendous optimism, a sense that there really is hope for true growth in characters. (This is also suggested—in fact foretold—in the opening illustration, where new life peeps blissfully in a nest made from Raphael's wig, a sign of his arrogance and vanity that had been stolen by birds. It suggests the triumph of the natural world, with all its simplicity and reality, over the hollowness and affectation of the world of the court.)

Perhaps the story's strongest theme is the equalizing power of love. Raphael searches for an equal without really believing that equality is possible. And in the way he seeks equality it is in fact not possible. Vanity, arrogance, and pride will not allow equality. Raphael must first learn the lessons of equality among friends. "Paws and hooves are no good for making fires and grinding flour and baking bread" (55), the Wolf tells Raphael, suggesting that equality does not mean that everyone is the same. Instead, equality affirms that all have a proper place, that none should be seen as more important or more significant than another. It is a startling lesson for Raphael, for he learns that equality, on the terms he had defined it, demands loneliness and isolation.

This lesson prepares him for the equality of marriage. When he come back to the palace, he at first comes sadly: "I have . . .

learned that I am not as handsome or clever or wealthy as I once thought. Indeed, my gracious lady, I have nothing to offer you but these goats, and they are yours already" (62). But now will come the completion of the lesson, for Raphael is quite wrong. He has one more thing to offer: himself. And this is what Rosamund takes, holding out her hand to him.

Love, Paterson suggests, is intimately tied to the ability to see beyond the self. It is tied to the ability to see another for his or her self, as equal in nature, not in mere appearance. Jess learns this about Leslie, Gilly about Trotter, Park about his grandfather, and Raphael about Rosamund. Although the lesson is learned through unconventional means, the story of *The King's Equal* closes absolutely conventionally: "They, and all in the land, lived happily together for many, many years" (62).

The World in 1492

The quincentennial anniversary of Columbus's arrival in the Americas was marked by a spate of books about that event. Many children's books published in 1992 express more than a little dismay at the effects of the intruding Western culture, and in this they followed the lead of many mainsteam texts that focus on the same event. *The World in 1492* came, perhaps unfortunately, during this sudden flow of Columbus books, but it took a profoundly different approach. Instead of focusing on the destruction of cultures, it avoids what it terms "Columbus bashing" and instead focuses on the rich tapestry of world history that is sometimes neglected in favor of this enormous first encounter. The text therefore examines five different parts of the world by dealing with what was happening in those cultures when Columbus set sail in 1492.

The work is an extraordinary collaboration, bringing together writers with cultural ties to each of the settings: Margaret Mahy on Australia and Oceania, Jean Fritz on Europe, Jamake Highwater on the Americas, Patricia and Fredrick McKissack on Africa, and Katherine Paterson on Asia. The five essays are marked by different approaches but each depicts those world events that were occurring while Columbus was sailing. The result is the depiction of an astonishing array of events, of empires rising and falling, of changes that will endure for centuries. The preface concludes that "when Columbus stops being the only story of 1492, more stories unfold than could possibly be contained in one book" (vi). That is perhaps the most important suggestion of the collection.

Paterson's selection on Asia deals with the cultures of the Middle East, China, Japan, Korea, Southeast Asia, and India, each in about three pages. Clearly these accounts are not meant to be exhaustive histories, but to explain the state of the culture in 1492 Paterson must establish earlier historical and cultural trends. Each section thus begins with that background, discussing the influences on that culture by other cultures and focusing particularly on the uniqueness of the culture. China is characterized principally as an isolating culture, Korea as a fusion of Buddhist and Confucian models, India as a source of "untold riches" for the rest of the world.

Paterson's essay opens with a focus on two characters, one Asian and one European. The pairing of Ghengis Khan with Marco Polo mirrors the clash of cultures represented by Columbus in the Americas. It also allows Paterson to focus on story, and she begins the essay with dramatic imagery:

> Silent but for the pounding of thousands upon thousands of hooves, nomad warriors thundered down the steppes of central Asia, changing the face of the world. These horsemen traveled twice as fast as any other army of the time. They never stopped riding. With his own remounts following him like obedient dogs, a warrior could switch horses as soon as the one he was riding grew weary. Each man carried dried milk and strips of beef in his saddlebag, and when those ran out, he would slit a vein in the leg of his horse and drink the blood. (33)

The images here are tactile, aural and visual. The gripping opening plunges the reader into a frenetic rush. It also suggests the importance of that rush—how that speedy army was to affect world history.

Paterson's conclusion returns to her opening, as she compares post-1492 contacts with those of Marco Polo: "The West . . . would come often to the ancient and great nations of Asia, but they did not come as Marco Polo had, in wonder and humility. For the next five hundred years they would come as conquerors and plunderers, too often seeking to destroy that which they did not understand" (65). And here is perhaps the piece's most important emphasis: the need to understand other cultures.

This piece represents a new direction for Paterson. She had of course written historical fiction, but she had not approached history for a child audience in this manner—as though she were writing *Lyddie* without Lyddie, or *Rebels of the Heavenly Kingdom* without Wang Lee and Mei Lin. The form does not sit easy with her, for to cover the history of such lands as China, Japan, India even superficially Paterson is forced to hold back on story in favor of facts. Her approach appears similar to that of historian Barbara Tuchman, but Paterson seems to abandon this approach in the face of the enormous amount of material to cover in just a few pages. She remains a storyteller: her history is the history of characters, and as much as possible she depicts characters as having stories.

Who Am I?

Paterson's most recent book is in one sense a new direction but in another a return to old forms. *Who Am I?* (1992) is a rewrite of Paterson's first book, composed at the request of the Presbyterian Church of America. In rewriting the text Paterson explicitly examines some of the questions she has implicitly examined in her novels since the 1966 publication of *Who Am I?*: "I love to write novels because they allow me to explore some of my deepest feelings with my readers. In these stories I have had a chance to ask some of life's hard questions: Why do people suffer and die? What happens when you let jealousy rule your life? Can love really change a person? Does my life matter?"[9] The first three questions appear prominently in *Bridge to Terabithia, Jacob Have I Loved,* and *The Great Gilly Hopkins.* But it is the final question dominates all of her novels: Do I matter? It is the question Muna poses, Goro poses, Wang Lee poses, Gilly is afraid to pose, Louise represses, and Lyddie desperately avoids.

The work is a devotional one, and beneath the questions is a solid affirmation: "For no matter how much my life has changed since I first wrote this book, the one thing that hasn't changed during these ever-changing years is the love and leading of God" (vii). With this assumption Paterson poses to young readers five basic questions about identity:

> Where in the world is God?
> What about me?
> Where do I belong?
> Who is my neighbor?
> What is my purpose?

What is most interesting about Paterson's approach to each question is her refusal to establish easy answers; she recognizes that each question itself opens up new questions. The first, for example, opens up the questions of pain and hurt, the unpredictability and seemingly wanton cruelty of the natural world, accidents with no apparent meaning, the possible discrepancy between a loving God and a broken world.

Her answers are meant to evoke rather than to limit; they open up ways of understanding. To the problems of evil and foolishness and the destructive abuse of creation, Paterson suggests that God could have taken away humanity's freedom and programmed it to abide by instinct alone, or He could have simply withdrawn from a created order in rebellion. But He did neither: "God has neither deserted us nor taken away our freedom and responsibility. Instead, God has chosen to complete the work or creation through us" (12). And there is the evocative response. What does it mean to "complete the work of creation through us"? To that there is no simple answer, but there is an approach—or a context—within which to understand the questions of pain and brokenness.

The themes Paterson has explored in her novels appear here as well. The theme of the family—and the explorations of its boundaries and nature—is especially prominent, as Paterson affirms here in a nonfictive guise that individuals must be themselves (as in *Jacob Have I Loved, Park's Quest,* and *Lyddie*) as well as parts of larger communities (as in *Of Nightingales That Weep, Rebels of the Heavenly Kingdom,* and *The Great Gilly Hopkins*). "Human beings, unlike many animals," Paterson writes, "need to belong to other people, and our families give us people to whom we belong and who belong to us" (35). She notes that this is not an easy belonging, and that there are many children who have no such belonging. But that does not change the essential need, the fundamental necessity of family. Certainly this is the conclusion both Park and Jimmy Jo come to: each is in tension with his family but recognizes the essential need of the family.

Paterson also affirms strongly the necessity of the individual. One of her subchapter headings suggests that people are "created to be and to belong" (20): "In the company of other people, a child can learn how to direct his or her own life and how to live with others. If this process breaks down, either because the child lacks loving adult care or because of some failures in the child to begin to take responsibility for his or her actions, the adult individual will be less than the person God intended" (21). People belong, but they are also individuals who take responsibility. This is a truth not lost on Gilly, who must come to recognize and accept the love that is offered, as well as see the sham of her fantasy. It is a truth not lost on Park, who must learn to see and understand the weaknesses of both his parents. And it is a truth not lost on Lyddie, who will go to Oberlin to "be," but who will return to "belong."

Paterson concludes the work with the question of purpose, and here she quotes the first answer of the Westminster Shorter Catechism: "Man's chief end is to glorify God, and to enjoy him forever." She responds to this, typically, with another question: "Is it possible that part of the meaning of life is for us to know this kind of pleasure in God's company?" (73). The catechism question is itself evocative: What does it mean to enjoy God? Though she speculates on this, she leaves the question as an approach, as is true of her novels. Do we enjoy God through our imaginations, like Jess and Leslie? Or through recognizing His hand in our lives, like Louise? Or in learning to extend and accept love, like Trotter and Gilly? Or by affirming good, though perhaps somewhat broken gifts, like Takiko and Park and Jimmy Jo? Or by planting seed corn, both metaphorically and physically, like Wang Lee and Mei Lin?

As in *The World in 1492,* Paterson uses story to convey ideas: "Because I am primarily a storyteller, I cannot seem to talk long without including a bit of a story" (vii–viii). Many of the questions Paterson poses can be abstract, so she grounds them in concrete story before she examines them. Here, for example, is the story of Lisa Hill, whose death made Paterson's son John question the nature of God. The stories Paterson poses suggest difficult situations, such as that of an apparently meaningless tragedy. But Paterson's reference to "a bit of a story" is significant. The stories appear only in part; as with her novels, Paterson withholds full and complete chronicling. Here many of the stories simply establish a situation. It is left to the reader to work out the stories' implications and meanings in the contexts of the questions Paterson poses.

Those who have read her novels will be familiar with the technique.

Conclusion: With the Child's Cooperation

In her essay "A Song of Innocence and Experience" Katherine Paterson addresses the question of whether she should be considered a didactic writer.

> When I write for the reader whose life I want to change, I am not writing for one of the beautiful people, but for one of the terrified—one of the "tired, the poor, the huddled masses, yearning to breathe free." If you must call me a didactic writer, go ahead. I do believe that those of us who have grown up have something of value to offer the young. And if that is didacticism, well, I have to live with it. But when I write a story, it is not an attempt to make children good or wise—nobody but God can do that, and even God doesn't do it without the child's cooperation. I am trying in a book to give children a place where they may find rest for their weary souls.[1]

Here is a passage that will send up all sorts of flags to moderns; it all sounds positively Victorian. Should a writer be about the business of changing lives? Should a writer be didactic? Aren't children, in all of their spontaneity and innocence, able to teach us adults? Isn't it the adults who have the weary souls and children who are as fresh as a sprig of heather? Shouldn't the proper adult role be one of nurturing the child along routes that the child is inclined to rather than plopping down knowledge and wisdom from on high?

To all of this Paterson seems impenitent. If one is to be a spy for hope, as she suggests in her novels, one brings to bear all of the experience that leads one to conclude that life must be lived in the context of hope. This does not mean, her novels assert, that life is easy; life is, in Trotter's word, "tough." It does not mean that life is a desert; it does mean, though, that life is rich. And Paterson feels very keenly that her role as a novelist for the child reader is to show the child that life is rich:

> We are not living in Nazi Germany, nor in a totalitarian state of the left or of the right. Not yet. But children have only so much time; the world has only so much time. We can't stop children from wasting time, but we don't have to abet it. We can, as far as it lies in our power to do so, offer them books which will nourish them in freedom, justice, and harmony; which will speak to their fears and widen their vision.[2]

In this sense the work of Katherine Paterson is indeed didactic. But what lends Paterson's work its power—in addition to its language, imagery, and deft characterization—is the fusion of story with teaching. The two are woven together in such a way as to make the story predominant, but the story carries with it the teaching—like Yohei's white and glowing cloth marked by a single blood-red line through it. Nancy Huse sees Paterson's work as being dominated by such a fusion: "Telling the truth in terms of her *zeit* as well as in reference to her private beliefs, Paterson writes stories of children who move from a state of flawed and bitter experience to one of coherence and insight about the ultimate nature of human life."[3] She concludes from this that it is difficult to place Paterson simply in the genre of realistic fiction—a difficulty that may seem specious at first glance. Certainly everything that happens in her novels is within the realm of the possible, therefore she must be seen as a realist. And yet, as Huse suggests, Paterson's goal of "telling the truth," of moving to "ultimate things," makes this categorization an uneasy one.

Paterson is uneasy with categorizations, though she feels comfortable with the label of children's writer. She has frequently been labeled a Christian writer, but there she feels less comfortable, preferring instead to be seen as a writer who is a Christian (Interview). Certainly one cannot read her essays in *Gates of Excellence* or *The Spying Heart* for very long without realizing that the Bible and her Christian, specifically Calvinist heritage strongly influences her notion of what humanity is all about. Her works vibrate to the Calvinist rhythms of fall and redemption, and the hope that she holds out to her child readers is quite distinctly a Christian hope:

> As a spiritual descendant of Moses, and the prophets and apostles who followed him, I have to think of hope in this context. We are not really optimists as the common definition goes, because we, like Moses, must be realistic about the world in which we find ourselves. And this world looked at squarely does not allow optimism to flourish. Hope for us cannot simply be wishful thinking, nor can it be only the desire to grow up and take control over our own lives. Hope is a yearning, rooted in reality, that pulls us toward the radical biblical vision of a world where truth and justice and peace do prevail, a time in which the knowledge of God will cover the earth as the waters cover the sea, a scene which finds humanity living in harmony with nature, all nations beating their swords into plowshares and walking together by the light of God's glory. Now there's a happy ending for you. The only purely happy ending I know of.[4]

It is hard to imagine other children's authors who are or have been so explicit about faith commitments. Perhaps only C. S. Lewis or Madeleine L'Engle come to mind. Certainly it is the case that if one is to understand the hope Paterson examines through her novels, and the hope that Paterson holds out to her readers, one must understand her biblical, Calvinist perspective.

Perhaps it is ironic that when Paterson's novels are attacked, they are more often than not attacked by Christian groups. *The Great Gilly Hopkins* has been attacked for its profanity, *Of Nightingales That Weep* for the marriage of a stepdaughter and stepfather, and *Bridge to Terabithia* for the crush that Jess has on Miss Edmunds and the scene in which Jess prays to spirits. Paterson seems aware of the possibility for offense as she describes some of her early novels:

> In the first, the hero is a bastard, and the chief female character ends up in a brothel. In the second, the heroine has an illicit love affair, her mother dies in a plague, and most of her com-

> panions commit suicide. In the third, which is full of riots in the streets, the hero's best friend is permanently maimed. In the fourth, a central child character dies in an accident. In the fifth, turning away from the mayhem in the first four, I wrote what I refer to as my "funny book." In it the heroine merely fights, lies, steals, cusses, bullies an emotionally disturbed child, and acts out her racial bigotry in a particularly vicious manner.[5]

Stated baldly, this does seem to be a line of novels filled with distress, anguish, and viciousness. But in fact each of these elements is placed in the context of hope. The bastard hero finds a true father, the heroine who finds illicit love also finds true love, the maiming of a protagonist's friend leads to the healing of two parent/child relationships, the death of one child leads to new life for another and others after him, and the stealing and cussing of Gilly give way to clouds of glory. Hope is a yearning rooted in reality, looking forward toward joy.

Paterson will be remembered for her powerful plots, but she will also be remembered for telling the truth about universal things. Her work is, as I suggested in the Preface, story woven with truth, so that the reader will know the place and the feeling. It is a bridge lovingly and expertly built, girded by the reality of a fallen world, and arching gracefully toward the Promised Land, for which she is a spy.

Notes and References

Preface

1. "Where Is Terabithia?" *Children's Literature Association Quarterly* 9 (Winter 1984–85): 157.

2. "National Book Award Acceptance," reprinted in part in *Gates of Excellence: On Reading and Writing Books for Children* (New York: Elsevier/Nelson, 1981), 109.

3. Interview with Katherine Paterson, 5 August 1992, Barre, Vermont, by Gary D. Schmidt and Anne Stickney Schmidt.

4. "Tell the Truth but Tell It Slant," in Betsy Hearne, ed., *The Zena Sutherland Lectures, 1983–1992* (New York: Clarion Books, 1993), 48–70.

1. Gathering Stories Along the Way

1. "National Book Award Acceptance," reprinted in part in *Gates of Excellence: On Reading and Writing Books for Children* (New York: Elsevier/Nelson, 1981), 109.

2. "Sounds in the Heart," *Horn Book* 57 (December 1981): 694–702; hereafter cited in text.

3. Interview with Katherine Paterson, 5 August 1992, Barre, Vermont, by Gary D. Schmidt and Anne Stickney Schmidt; hereafter cited in text as "Interview."

4. "Heart in Hiding," in William Zinsser, ed., *Worlds of Childhood: The Art and Craft of Writing for Children* (Boston: Houghton Mifflin, 1990), 161.

5. Jean Fritz, *Homesick: My Own Story* (New York: G. P. Putnam, 1982).

6. Virginia Buckley, "Katherine Paterson," *Horn Book* 54 (August 1978): 370; hereafter cited in text.

7. "Up from Elsie Dinsmore," in *Gates of Excellence,* 100; hereafter cited in text as "Dinsmore."

8. "Before the Gates of Excellence," in *Gates of Excellence,* 2; hereafter cited in text as "Excellence."

9. "Words," in *Gates of Excellence,* 8; hereafter cited in text as "Words."

10. *Justice for All People* (New York: Friendship Press, 1973).

11. "The Aim of the Writer Who Writes for Children," *Theory into Practice* 31, no. 4 (Autumn 1982): 327–28; hereafter cited in text as "Aim."

12. "Newbery Award Acceptance," *Horn Book* 54 (August 1978): 364–65; hereafter cited in text as "Newbery."

13. "Where Is Terabithia?" *Children's Literature Association Quarterly* 9 (Winter 1984–85): 153–57.

14. William W. Warner, *Beautiful Swimmers: Watermen, Crabs and the Chesapeake Bay* (Boston: Little, Brown, 1976).

15. "The Secret Life of Katherine Clements Womeldorf," in *Once upon a Time: Celebrating the Magic in Children's Books in Honor of the Twentieth Anniversary of Reading Is Fundamental* (New York: Putnam, 1986), 18–19.

16. Thomas Pettepiece and Anatoly Aleksin, eds., *Face to Face* (New York: Philomel Books, 1990).

17. Jean Fritz, Katherine Paterson, Patricia and Fredrick McKissack, Margaret Mahy, and Jamake Highwater, *The World in 1492* (New York: Henry Holt & Co., 1992); hereafter cited in text.

18. John Paterson and Katherine Paterson, *Consider the Lilies* (New York: Thomas Y. Crowell, 1986), 12–13.

19. Ray Bradbury, "Memories Shape the Voice," in Charlotte F. Otten and Gary D. Schmidt, eds., *The Voice of the Narrator in Children's Literature* (New York: Greenwood Press, 1989), 132.

2. The Search for Hope: The Early Historical Fiction

1. *The Sign of the Chrysanthemum* (New York: Lippincott and Crowell, 1973), 130; hereafter cited in text.

2. Christopher Wordsworth, "Broken Boughs," *New Statesman,* 23 May 1975, 698.

3. Review of *The Sign of the Chrysanthemum, Publishers Weekly,* 10 December 1973, 36.

4. Virginia Haviland, review of *The Sign of the Chrysanthemum, Horn Book* 49 (October 1973): 468; hereafter cited in text.

5. Graham Hammond, "Feminine Insights," *Times Literary Supplement,* 19 September 1975, 1056.

6. Elements of the ceremonious nature of Fukuji's character come from Paterson's reading of Robert Newman's *The Japanese: People of the*

Treasures (New York: Atheneum, 1964), which describes the Japanese swordmaker (104–16). The work also includes the well-known anecdote of the apprentice to the swordsman who found that his apprenticeship involved exclusively what Muna would call "woman's work." This apprentice, like Muna, finds such work is actually preparation for the true apprenticeship (137–38).

7. *Of Nightingales That Weep* (New York: Thomas Y. Crowell, 1974), 170; hereafter cited in text.

8. *The Master Puppeteer* (New York: Thomas Y. Crowell, 1975), 44; hereafter cited in text.

9. "Why Do I Write?" Promotional material for Lodestar Books, n.d.

10. "Do I Dare Disturb the Universe?" *Horn Book* 60 (September–October 1984): 642.

11. *Rebels of the Heavenly Kingdom* (New York: E. P. Dutton, 1983), 227; hereafter cited in text.

12. M. Sarah Smedman, "Out of the Depths to Joy: Spirit/Soul in Juvenile Novels," in Francelia Butler and Richard Rotert, eds., *Triumphs of the Spirit in Children's Literature* (Hamden, Conn.: Library Professional Publications, 1986), 195.

3. Prodigal Children in Search of Hope

1. *Bridge to Terabithia* (New York: HarperCollins, 1977), 128; hereafter cited in text.

2. *The Great Gilly Hopkins* (New York: Thomas Y. Crowell, 1978), 52; hereafter cited in text.

3. Paterson's use of these lines is multidimensional, suggesting Gilly's many layers of understanding. See M. Sarah Smedman's argument along these lines in "When Literary Works Meet: Allusion in the Novels of Katherine Paterson," in Susan R. Gannon and Ruth Anne Thompson, eds., *Where Rivers Meet: Confluence and Concurrents: Selected Papers from the 1989 International Conference of the Children's Literature Association* (New York: Pace University, 1989), 59–66; hereafter cited in text.

4. Cited in Gene Inyart Namovicz, "Katherine Paterson," *Horn Book* 57 (August 1981): 394–99.

5. Trotter's sentiments here seem to have been important right from the beginning of the novel's construction. They appear in an early manuscript as ideas jotted down on the back of an envelope, held today among Paterson's papers in the Kerlan Collection of the University of Minnesota, Minneapolis: "It's like a bad secret we think we can keep from children and they always find out. It ain't bad unless you make it that way yourself, but it's tough" (cited in Smedman, 61).

6. Claudia Mills, "Children in Search of a Family: Orphan Novels through the Century," *Children's Literature in Education* 18 (Winter 1989): 227–39.

7. *Angels and Other Strangers* (New York: Thomas Y. Crowell, 1979), 25; hereafter cited in text.

8. *Jacob Have I Loved* (New York: HarperCollins, 1980), 35; hereafter cited in text.

9. Smedman continues this argument in "'A Good Oyster': Story and Meaning in *Jacob Have I Loved*," *Children's Literature in Education* 14 (Autumn 1983): 180–87, which focuses on Louise's withdrawal. James Holt McGavran, Jr., attacks this position in "Bathrobes and Bibles, Waves and Words in Katherine Paterson's *Jacob Have I Loved*," *Children's Literature in Education* 17 (Spring 1986): 3–15, where he argues that the reconciliation suggested by Smedman never takes place, that instead it is too late, that Louise is irrevocably trapped in her adolescent and adult lives. McGavran makes no allowance in his argument for the limited narrative point of view, so that his assessment of the context of Louise's trap is never made apart from Louise's perspective.

10. Caroline Goforth, "The Role of the Island in *Jacob Have I Loved*," *Children's Literature Association Quarterly* 9 (Winter 1984–85): 176–78.

4. Exploring the Boundaries of the Family

1. *Come Sing, Jimmy Jo* (New York: E. P. Dutton, 1985), 10; hereafter cited in text.

2. Geraldine DeLuca and Roni Natov, "The State of the Field in Contemporary Children's Fantasy: An Interview with George Woods," *Lion and the Unicorn* 1, no. 2 (1977): 5–6.

3. *Park's Quest* (New York: E. P. Dutton, 1988), 5–6; hereafter cited in text.

4. David Staines, trans., *The Complete Romances of Chrétien de Troyes* (Bloomington: Indiana University Press, 1990), 340.

5. John Hayward, *The New England Gazetteer* (Boston: John Hayward, 1839), unpaged.

6. Benita Eisler, *The Lowell Offering: Writings by New England Mill Women (1840–45)* (New York: Harper & Row, 1977). This collection was reviewed in *Horn Book* 54 (August 1978): 429; it followed Paterson's acceptance speech for the Newbery Award for *Bridge to Terabithia*.

7. Harriet Hanson Robinson, *Loom and Spindle; or, Life among the Early Mill Girls* (New York: Thomas Y. Crowell, 1898).

8. *Lyddie* (New York: E. P. Dutton, 1991), 45; hereafter cited in text.

9. Elizabeth S. Watson, review of *Lyddie*, *Horn Book* 67 (May–June 1991): 339.

10. Natalie Babbitt, review of *Lyddie, New York Times Book Review,* 19 May 1991, 24.

11. Charles Dickens, *Hard Times,* ed. George Ford and Sylvhre Monod (New York: Norton, 1966), 17.

5. New Directions and Old Forms

1. Sumiko Yagawa, *The Crane Wife,* trans. Katherine Paterson (New York: Mulberry Books, 1987); hereafter cited in text.

2. Momoko Ishii, *The Tongue-cut Sparrow,* trans. Katherine Paterson (New York: E. P. Dutton, 1987); hereafter cited in text.

3. *The Tale of the Mandarin Ducks* (New York: E. P. Dutton, 1990); hereafter cited in text.

4. Juliet Piggot, *Japanese Mythology* (New York: Peter Bedrick Books, 1982), 115.

5. *The Smallest Cow in the World* (New York: Harper Collins, 1991), 58–64; hereafter cited in text.

6. Jack Zipes, review of *The King's Equal, New York Times Book Review,* 15 November 1992, 27; hereafter cited in text.

7. Pettepiece and Aleksin, eds., *Face to Face.* The selection from *Park's Quest* is taken from chapter 3 and describes Park's visit to the Vietnam War Memorial (pp. 197–202).

8. *The King's Equal* (New York: HarperCollins, 1992), 11; hereafter cited in text.

9. *Who Am I?* (Grand Rapids: Eerdman's Publishers, 1992), vii; hereafter cited in text.

Conclusion

1. "A Song of Innocence and Experience," in *Gates of Excellence,* 49.

2. "Living in a Peaceful World," *Horn Book* 67 (January–February, 1991): 38.

3. Nancy Huse, "Katherine Paterson's Ultimate Realism," *Children's Literature Association Quarterly* 9 (Fall 1984): 99.

4. "Hope Is More than Happiness," *New York Times Book Review,* 25 December 1988, 19.

5. "Creativity Limited: Novels for Young People Today," in *Gates of Excellence,* 34.

Selected Bibliography

Primary Works

Fiction

Angels and Other Strangers: Family Christmas Stories. New York: Crowell, 1979. Published in Great Britain as *Star of Night.* London: Gollancz, 1980.

Bridge to Terabithia. New York: Crowell, 1977.

Come Sing, Jimmy Jo. New York: Dutton, 1985.

Consider the Lilies: Plants of the Bible. With John Paterson. New York: Crowell, 1986.

The Crane Wife (translator). Sumiko Yagawa, reteller. New York: Morrow, 1981.

Flip-Flop Girl. New York: Lodestar Books, 1994.

The Great Gilly Hopkins. New York: Crowell, 1978.

Jacob Have I Loved. New York: Crowell, 1980.

The King's Equal. New York: HarperCollins, 1992.

Lyddie. New York: Dutton, 1991.

The Master Puppeteer. New York: Crowell, 1976.

Of Nightingales That Weep. New York: Crowell, 1974.

Park's Quest. New York: Dutton, 1988.

Rebels of the Heavenly Kingdom. New York: Dutton, 1983.

The Sign of the Chrysanthemum. New York: Crowell, 1973.

The Smallest Cow in the World. New York: HarperCollins, 1991.

The Tale of the Mandarin Ducks. New York: Dutton, 1990.

The Tongue-cut Sparrow (translator). Momoko Ishii, reteller. New York: Dutton, 1987.

Nonfiction

"Asia in 1492." In Jean Fritz, Katherine Paterson, Patricia and Fredrick McKissack, Margaret Mahy, and Jamake Highwater, *The World in 1492.* New York: Henry Holt, 1992.

Gates of Excellence: On Reading and Writing Books for Children. New York: Elsevier/Nelson, 1981.
Justice for All People. New York: Friendship Press, 1973.
The Spying Heart: More Thoughts on Reading and Writing Books for Children. New York: Dutton, 1989.
To Make Men Free. Richmond, Va.: John Knox Press, 1973.
Who Am I? Richmond, Va.: Covenant Life Curriculum; John Knox Press 1966. Revised and reprinted, Grand Rapids, Mich.: Eerdmans Publishers, 1992.

Essays on Children's Literature

"The Aim of the Writer Who Writes for Children." *Theory into Practice* 31, no. 4 (Autumn 1982): 325–31.
"Daughters of Hope." *Horn Book* 68 (March–April, 1992): 164–70.
"Do I Dare Disturb the Universe?" *Horn Book* 60 (September–October, 1984): 640–51.
"Heart in Hiding." In William Zinsser, ed., *Worlds of Childhood: The Art and Craft of Writing for Children,* 147–77. Boston: Houghton Mifflin, 1990.
"Hope and Happy Endings." Plenary Address. Fourth Biennial Conference on Literature and Hawaii's Children. In Christina Bacchilega and Steven Curry, eds., *Literature and Hawaii's Children. Imagination: A Bridge to Magic Realms in the Humanities,* 146–55. Honolulu: Literature and Hawaii's Children, 1990.
"Hope Is More than Happiness." *New York Times Book Review,* 25 December 1988, 19.
"Living in a Peaceful World." *Horn Book* 67 (January–February, 1991): 32–38.
"National Book Award Acceptance." *Horn Book* 55 (August 1979): 402–403.
"Newbery Award Acceptance." *Horn Book* 54 (August 1978): 361–67.
"Newbery Award Acceptance." *Horn Book* 57 (August 1981): 385–93.
"Only a Lamp-Holder: On Writing Historical Fiction." In Barbara Harrison and Gregory Maguire, eds., *Innocence and Experience: Essays and Conversations on Children's Literature,* 263–64. New York: Lothrop, Lee & Shepard, 1987.
"The Perilous Realms." A colloquy in which Katherine Paterson participates. In Barbara Harrison and Gregory Maguire, eds., *Innocence and Experience: Essays and Conversations on Children's Literature,* 195–209. New York: Lothrop, Lee, & Shepard, 1987.
"The Secret Life of Katherine Clements Womeldorf." *In Once upon a Time: Celebrating the Magic of Children's Books in Honor of the*

Twentieth Anniversary of Reading is Fundamental, 18–19. New York: Putnam, 1986.
"Sounds in the Heart." *Horn Book* 57 (December, 1981): 694–702.
"Stick to Reality and a Dream." Washington, D.C.: Children's Literature Center, 1991.
"*The Tale of the Mandarin Ducks:* Beauty and the Beast." *Horn Book* 68 (January–February, 1992): 32–34.
"Tales of a Reluctant Dragon." *New Advocate* 2, no. 1 (Winter, 1989): 1–8.
"Tell the Truth but Tell It Slant." In Betsy Hearne, ed., *The Zena Sutherland Lectures, 1983–1992,* 48–70. New York: Clarion Books, 1993.
"Wednesday's Children." *Horn Book* 63 (May–June, 1986): 287–94.
"What Writing Has Taught Me." *Writer,* August 1990, 9–10.
"Where Is Terabithia?" *Children's Literature Association Quarterly* 9 (Winter 1984–85): 153–57.
"Why Do I Write?" Promotional material for *Rebels of the Heavenly Kingdom.* New York: Lodestar Books, n.d.

Secondary Works

Biographical Studies

Buckley, Virginia. "Katherine Paterson." *Horn Book* 54 (August 1978): 368–71.
Haskell, Ann. "Talk with a Winner." *New York Times Book Review,* 26 April 1981, 52, 67–68.
Jones, Linda T. "Profile Katherine Paterson." *Language Arts* 58 (February 1981): 189–96.
"Katherine Paterson Named Recipient of the 1983 Medallion." *Juvenile Miscellany* 13, no. 3 (Winter 1983): 1–3.
Namovicz, Gene Inyart. "Katherine Paterson." *Horn Book* 57 (August 1981): 394–99.

Critical Studies

Baer, Elizabeth R. "Books as Bridges: The Tradition of the Child Reader in Katherine Paterson's *Bridge to Terabithia.*" In Christina Bacchilega and Steven Curry, eds., *Literature and Hawaii's Children. Imagination: A Bridge to Magic Realms in the Humanities,* 63–72. Honolulu: Literature and Hawaii's Children, 1990. Focusing on

Park's Quest and *Bridge to Terabithia,* this article examines the effects of reading on literary characters.

Bell, Anthea. "A Case of Commitment." *Signal* 38 (May 1982): 73–81. Comments on the Christian elements in Paterson's work.

Chaston, Joel D. "Flute Solos and Songs That Make You Shatter: Simple Melodies in *Jacob Have I Loved* and *Come Sing, Jimmy Jo.*" *Lion and the Unicorn* 16 (1992): 215–22. Reviews the use of music as a thematic device in two of Paterson's novels.

———. "The Other Deaths in *Bridge to Terabithia.*" *Children's Literature Association Quarterly* 16 (Winter 1991–92): 238–41. Focuses on Leslie's death as well on the metaphorical deaths which are connected to it.

Curry, Steven. "Fate and Friendship: Lessons of Loss in *Bridge to Terabithia* and *Charlotte's Web.*" In Christina Bacchilega and Steven Curry, eds., *Literature and Hawaii's Children. Imagination: A Bridge to Magic Realms in the Humanities;* 96–100. Honolulu: Literature and Hawaii's Children, 1990. Examines the role of the imagination in helping child readers cope with the knowledge of mortality.

Goforth, Caroline. "The Role of the Island in *Jacob Have I Loved.*" *Children's Literature Association Quarterly* 9, no. 4 (Winter 1984–85): 176–78. Compares the shrinking of Rass to the shrinking of Louise into herself, noting that the island is a place that is isolated and is isolating.

Gough, John. "*Bridge to Terabithia*: The Subtlety of Plain Language." *Idiom* 18 (Summer 1983): 19–22. Describes the many levels of meaning that Paterson achieves in the language of *Bridge to Terabithia,* despite that language's apparent simplicity.

Huse, Nancy. "Katherine Paterson's Ultimate Realism." *Children's Literature Association Quarterly* 9 (Fall 1984): 99–101. Proposes that the power of Paterson's work comes through the fusion of realism and idealism.

Jameson, Gloria. "Developing Self-Identity through Religious Consciousness in Stories of George MacDonald, C. S. Lewis, Madeleine L'Engle, Katherine Paterson, Ursula LeGuin, and Laura Adams Armer." *Hawaii 3: Literature and Hawaii's Children,* 143–47. Honolulu: Literature and Hawaii's Children, 1988. A broad examination of growth in the context of a Christian consciousness.

Kimmel, Eric A. "Beyond Death: Children's Books and the Hereafter." *Horn Book* 56 (June 1980): 265–73. In discussing the ways in which children's novels have dealt the the subject of death, this article deals with *Bridge to Terabithia.*

———. "Trials and Revelations: Katherine Paterson's Heroic Journeys." *New Advocate* 3, no. 4 (Fall 1990): 235–45. Explores Joseph Campbell's myth of the heroic by examining its effect on Paterson's novels.

McGavran, James H., Jr. "Bathrobes and Bibles, Waves and Words in Katherine Paterson's *Jacob Have I Loved.*" *Children's Literature in Education* 17 (Spring 1986): 3–15. Suggests that Louise's entrapment is not alleviated by any reconciliation at the end of the novel but is in fact something that carries over into her adult life.

Mills, Claudia. "Children in Search of a Family: Orphan Novels through the Century." *Children's Literature in Education* 18, no. 4 (Winter 1987): 227–39. Places *The Great Gilly Hopkins* in the genre of novels dealing with the experience of orphans, comparing Paterson's novel most especially to *Anne of Green Gables.*

Nist, Joan. "Archetypal Strands in Katherine Paterson's Novels of the Orient." In Christina Bacchilega and Steven Curry, eds., *Literature and Hawaii's Children. Imagination: A Bridge to Magic Realms in the Humanities,* 25–29. Honolulu: Literature and Hawaii's Children, 1990. Examines the four works of historical fiction set in Japan and China, noting that the archetypal activities of the protagonists render them universal rather than particular.

Powers, Douglas. "Of Time, Place, and Person: *The Great Gilly Hopkins* and Problems of Story for Adopted Children." *Children's Literature in Education* 15 (Winter 1984): 211–19. An examination from the point of view of a child psychologist of peer readings of *The Great Gilly Hopkins* and how adopted children react to the novel.

Rees, David. "The Wound of Philoctetes." In David Rees, *What Do Draculas Do? Essays on Contemporary Writers of Fiction for Children and Young Adults,* 222–34. Metuchen, N.J.: Scarecrow Press, 1990. First published as "On Katherine Paterson, Alexander Pope, Myself, and Some Others." *Children's Literature in Education* 14, no. 3 (Autumn 1983): 160–70. While examining the presence of Christianity in Paterson's novels and *Gates of Excellence,* the article explores why certain kinds of passages are judged to be problematic in children's literature.

Smedman, M. Sarah. "'A Good Oyster': Story and Meaning in *Jacob Have I Loved.*" *Children's Literature in Education* 14, no. 3 (Autumn 1983): 180–87. Focusing on Louise, the article suggests makes a comparison between Louise and the closed oysters she dredges up from the bay, noting that Louise closes herself off from her world.

———. "Not Always Gladly Does She Teach, nor Gladly Learn: Teachers in *Künsterinroman* for Young Readers." *Children's Literature in Education* 20, no. 3 (September 1989): 131–49. Among other novels, this focuses on the teacher relationship in *The Great Gilly Hopkins.*

———. "Out of the Depths to Joy: Spirit/Soul in Juvenile Novels." In Francelia Butler and Richard Rotert, eds., *Triumphs of the Spirit in Children's Literature,* 181–97. Hamden, Conn.: Library Professional Publications, 1986. In examining stories in which the triumph of the human spirit suggests a religious experience, this article examines the union of spirit and soul in *Rebels of the Heavenly Kingdom.*

———. "The Quest for the Father in the Fiction of Katherine Paterson." In Christina Bacchilega and Steven Curry, eds., *Literature and Hawaii's Children. Imagination: A Bridge to Magic Realms in the Humanities,* 30–39. Honolulu: Literature and Hawaii's Children, 1990. Examination of the search for the father in *Of Nightingales That Weep* and *Come Sing, Jimmy Jo.*

———. "The Quest for the Father in Katherine Paterson's *Of Nightingales That Weep.*" In Susan R. Ganon and Ruth Ann Thompson, eds., *The Child and the Family: Selected Papers from the 1988 International Conference of the Children's Literature Association,* 59–64. New York: Pace University, 1990. Deals with Paterson's metaphorical use of the search for a father as a structural device in the novel.

———. "Springs of Hope: Recovery of Primordial Time in 'Mythic' Novels for Young Readers." *Children's Literature* 16 (1988): 91–107. Examnes the role of hope in a historical context in *Rebels of the Heavenly Kingdom.*

———. "When Literary Works Meet: Allusion in the Novels of Katherine Paterson." In Susan R. Ganon and Ruth Anne Thompson, eds., *Where Rivers Meet: Confluence and Concurrents, Selected Papers from the 1989 International Conference of the Children's Literature Association,* 59–65. New York: Pace University, 1989. Deals with paterson's use of literary allusion as a narrative device, particularly in *The Great Gilly Hopkins.*

Index

The Author

Gary D. Schmidt received his B.A. from Gordon College, Wenham, Massachusetts, and his M.A. and Ph.D. in medieval literature from the University of Illinois at Urbana-Champaign. A professor of English at Calvin College, Grand Rapids, Michigan, he teaches children's literature, medieval and Renaissance literature, and the history of the English language. He has co-edited two collections of essays by children's literature critics and authors: *The Voice of the Narrator in Children's Literature* (1989), with Charlotte F. Otten, and *Sitting at the Feet of the Past: The Retelling of the North American Folktale* (1992), with Donald R. Hettinga. The author of *Robert McCloskey* (1990) and *Hugh Lofting* (1992), Schmidt has ventured into the writing children's literature with the retelling of *Pilgrim's Progress* (1994), illustrated by Barry Moser.

The Editor

Ruth K. MacDonald is associate dean of Bay Path College. She received her B.A. and M.A. in English from the University of Connecticut, her Ph.D. in English from Rutgers University, and her M.B.A. from the University of Texas at El Paso. To Twayne's United States and English Authors series she has contributed the volumes on Louisa May Alcott, Beatrix Potter, and Dr. Seuss. She is also the author of *Literature for Children in England and America, 1646-1774* (1982).